THE TRIALS AND TRIBULATIONS OF DORA SCHINTZ
HER JOURNEY FROM WEALTHY PHILANTHROPIST
TO BANKRUPT AND HOMELESS SPINSTER

JOHN ATHERSUCH

ISBN: 978-1-914934-63-6

Published 2023 by Peacock Press, Scout Bottom Farm, Mytholmroyd, Hebden Bridge, West Yorkshire, HX7 5JS.

Author's address:

17 The Bothy, Ottershaw Park,
Chobham Road, Ottershaw,
Surrey, KT16 0QG, UK

Text and photos copyright © John Athersuch 2023.

All rights reserved. No part of this publication may be reproduced, stored in a retrieval system or transmitted in any form or by any means without prior permission in writing from the author.

Further copies available from the publisher or the author.

Front cover illustration: Colourised photograph of Dora Schintz courtesy Annabel Collenette.

Book © Peacock Press. Book design by www.SiPat.co.uk

THE TRIALS AND TRIBULATIONS OF DORA SCHINTZ

HER JOURNEY FROM WEALTHY PHILANTHROPIST TO BANKRUPT AND HOMELESS SPINSTER

JOHN ATHERSUCH

FOREWORD

Local history can lead in surprising directions and uncover extraordinary stories. Just over ten years ago, John Athersuch researched and published the history of his home, Ottershaw Park in Surrey. It was a tremendous achievement, charting the fortunes of the house and its owners over the course of 250 years. Through careful research at Surrey History Centre and a host of other archive and local studies collections across the country, John vividly brought to life the people associated with Ottershaw throughout its history until its sale in 1930 amidst the bankruptcy of the extraordinary Miss Schintz, its last owner. Of all Ottershaw's private owners, it was Miss Schintz who proved the most tantalising and demanding of further research.

Born in 1868 into extraordinary wealth founded upon mineral mining in Chile and a fertilizer plant in France but leaving an estate of under £2,000 on her lonely death in 1954, Dora Schintz lived a life of extremes. High society balls, horse-breeding and national equestrian competitions, fast cars and sustained generous philanthropy contrasted sharply with personal frugality, ferocious litigiousness and a surprising financial naivety that ultimately led to bankruptcy and isolation in a residential hotel. A self-confessed loner, she remains an enigma.

I well remember John sharing with me his frustration that, despite his best efforts, she was proving to be so very elusive; and yet his meticulous research, based on thorough use of estate records, legal proceedings, a rich seam of family records and the amazing resources of online newspaper archives finally allows us to understand the life of this paradoxical woman.

Dora Schintz evades our gaze in the opulent portrait brought so vividly to life in colour on the front of this book. She avoided publicity, looking awkward in the 'special picture' of her that was printed in the *Daily Mail* in 1932 and icily remote in a later photograph printed by the *Daily Express* in 1937; and yet in John's company we can at last follow the turbulent course of her fascinating life, in a biography that is an enormous pleasure to read. Local history is about people, and archives are often the scattered remains of their lives and stories. I am delighted that John never gave up on Miss Schintz and has been able to piece together her remarkable story.

Julian Pooley F.S.A
Heritage Public Services and Engagement Manager
Surrey History Centre
March 2023

PREFACE

I first learned about Dora Schintz (1868 - 1954) when I was documenting the history of Ottershaw Park in Surrey. To my mind, she was one of the most interesting owners of the estate. Curiosity got the better of me and my research into her life extended beyond her brief period of residence at Ottershaw. In my quest to find out ever more about this intriguing woman my research has taken me to numerous archives to explore such diverse subjects as hackney horses[1], court proceedings, Companies House records and newspaper articles. I have also received support and encouragement in my endeavours from some of her distant relatives.

One of the most difficult problems I encountered in writing this biography was the lack of information about the first 40 years of her life. At one point I even thought of titling this book *Volume 2* in the hope that later I would be able to fill a *Volume 1* with new insights into her early life. I realise now that this is not likely to happen and that, until she burst on the hackney horse scene in the early 1900s, Dora presumably led a fairly unremarkable life in her family home in Liverpool.

The *Trials and Tribulations* of the title reflects the many legal battles that Dora was involved in throughout her life. Accounts of these cases in court records and in the press provided much of the information I have been able to gather about her.

ACKNOWLEDGEMENTS

I am indebted to the following:

Annabel Collenette and the late Sheila Collenette for sharing family photographs and heirlooms.

Robert Freeman for copies of Dora's letters and photographs.

Mario von Moos for genealogical information on the Schinz family.

Tom Clarke for his encyclopaedic knowledge of automobiles.

Jonathon Wild for his help on Childwall Hall and colourisation.

Robin Leach, John Fasal and Ann Ansell for photographs.

Glyn Hughes, Honorary Archivist of the Alpine Club, London for searching their records on my behalf.

Dawn Hicketts of the Hackney Society for help with hackney horses.

Robert Bachelor for access to material in the University of Reading Library.

The staff of Surrey History Centre, Woking, Cambridge University Library, Warwickshire County Record Office, Lewes Record Office, Liverpool Record

Office, The British Library, The National Archives, The Oliver Collection, Royal Holloway University of London, Chertsey Museum, Chertsey Library, Staatsarchiv des Kantons Zurich, Stadtarchiv Zürich, Zentralbibliothek Zürich, Kent County Crematorium, Woking Crematorium, Girlings, Canterbury, C.W. Lyons & Son, Canterbury and Christ Church, Ottershaw.

British Library Newspapers (formerly the Newspaper Library at Colindale) and online newspaper archives.

Jeremy Burbidge, Peacock Press, is thanked for his advice and assistance with publishing.

Special thanks to Sheila Binns for casting her critical eye over a draft of this book and making suggestions for improvement and to Julian Pooley (Surrey History Centre) for providing a Foreword.

Last but not least, my wife, Carol, for sharing the thrill of each new discovery with me!

Where appropriate I have referred in the text to the sources of information I have used in this study. I apologise to those whose help I have omitted to acknowledge and thank them for their contribution. Where any possibility of copyright exists, attempts have been made to contact the owners to obtain permission to publish and I am grateful to those who waived fees. If I have inadvertently infringed someone's copyright, I hope that I will be excused in the cause of promoting an interest in history. All unattributed images are the property of the author.

INTRODUCTION

It was while I was researching my book *The History of Ottershaw Park Estate 1761 - 2011* that I became intrigued by the life story of the last private owner of the estate, Dora Schintz. Dora came from a family of great wealth and through an inheritance became rich beyond most people's wildest dreams. She made a name for herself in the world of hackney horse competitions winning many prestigious prizes. She did not seek fame and gave generously to the needy, particularly through funding hospitals and homes for incurables. However, much of her fortune was quickly lost through being swindled by mortgagees and through ill-advised loans to an entrepreneur, Frederick Lionel Rapson, and she was later declared bankrupt. She spent the final years of her life trying to recoup her losses and defended Rapson's reputation to the last despite him being instrumental in her financial downfall. She died alone with little to her name and no-one to attend her funeral.

NOBLE ANCESTRY

Before looking at the life of Dora Schintz, it is worth exploring her family background and ancestry among the Swiss nobility. Schinz [sic] is an ancient Swiss family name which can be traced back at least as far as Hans Schinz, born in Zurich in 1547. The 't' in Schintz was added by Dora's father presumably for ease of pronunciation by the English. Nevertheless, Dora persisted in signing her name without the "t".

Among the Schintz family heirlooms are detailed hand painted heraldic *seize quartiers* showing the noble ancestry of both of Dora's great-great-grandparents, Hans Kaspar Schinz (b.1727) and his wife Anna Escher (d.1805), who were married in 1752.

A seize quartiers (sixteen quarters) is a heraldic display demonstrating that all of an individual's great-great-grandparents were entitled to bear arms in their own right. They were used as a proof of nobility most particularly in continental Europe in the 17th and 18th centuries. Possession of seize quartiers guaranteed admission to any court in Europe and bestowed many advantages. The design of both the Schinz and Escher seize quartiers is unusual in that they both present thirty-two armigerous ancestors rather than the usual sixteen. The Schinz coat of arms is described as '*Azure, issuant out of a crescent in base or, two ostrich feathers argent, in chief a mullet of six points of the second*'[2] and the crest depicts what appears to be a jester holding a crescent moon in his right hand and a star in his left. The symbolic significance of this crest, if any, is not known.

Seize quartieres of Hans Kaspar Schinz born 14th June 1727

Annabel Collenette

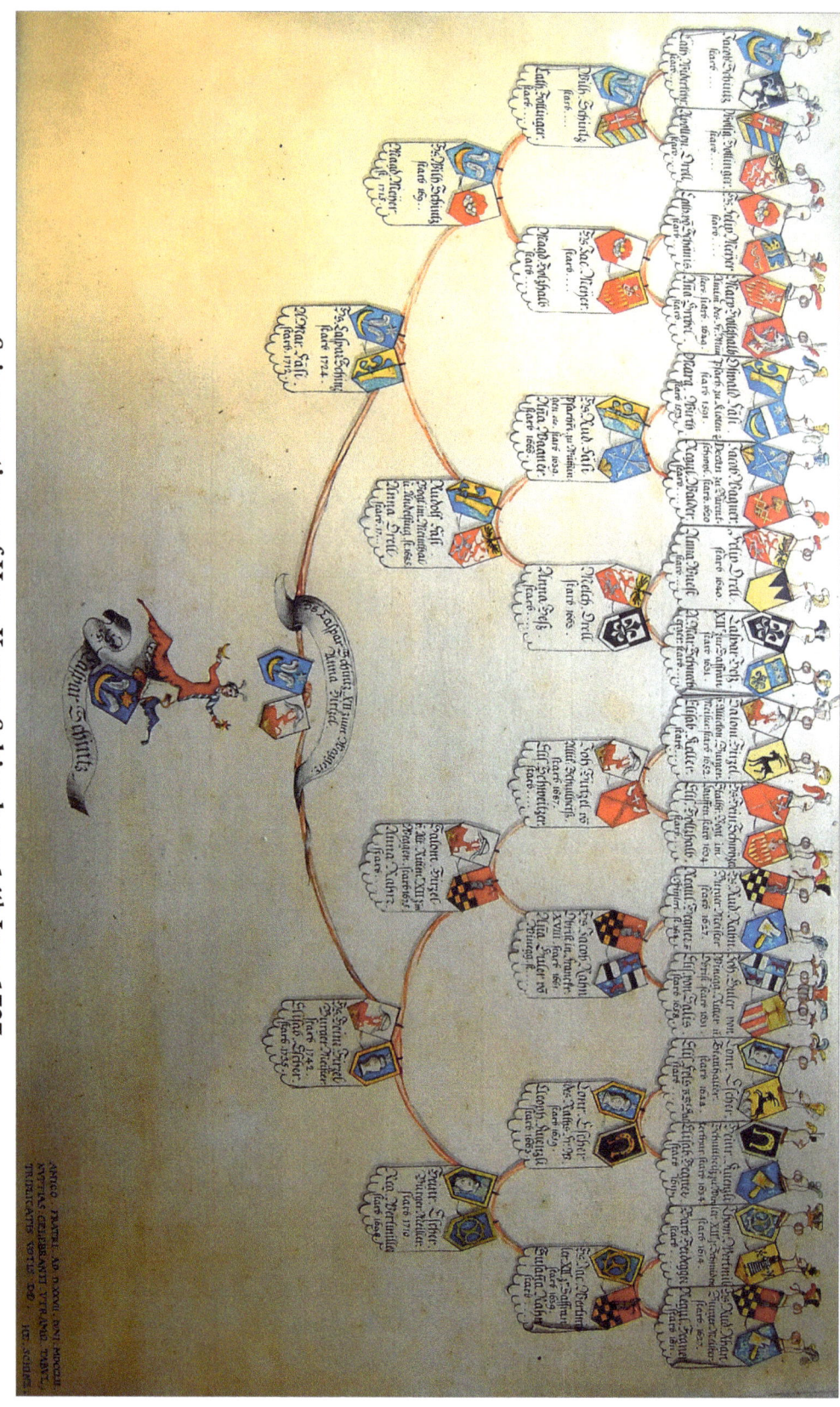

DORA'S FAMILY

Dora's father, Johann Kaspar (otherwise Hans Gaspard) Schintz (1837 - 1912) was the great grandson of the Hans Kaspar referred to above. He was a Swiss citizen born in Zurich but settled in Liverpool in about 1862 where he shared lodgings with a Frenchman called Paul Frederic Reyher. The two of them soon set up in business as Reyher & Schintz, a partnership which lasted until 1877 when it was dissolved by mutual consent. In 1864 Hans Gaspard married Anna Julia Bleuler (1843 - 1921) in Zurich and became a naturalised British subject in 1875. Reyher, had in the meantime become a British citizen in 1869.

Hans Gaspard was a well-known and highly esteemed personality in Liverpool and subscribed generously to many local charities, and in an unobtrusive way carried out many generous acts.

By the end of the 19th century, Liverpool had become a truly cosmopolitan city, second only to London in trade and commerce. Against this background Hans Gaspard became a very wealthy commission merchant with offices in Manchester Buildings, Tithebarn Street, located in the heart of Liverpool's business district, where he traded as Schintz & Co. between 1881 and 1912.

Hans Gaspard Schintz and his wife Anna Julia (née Bleuler)
Annabel Collenette

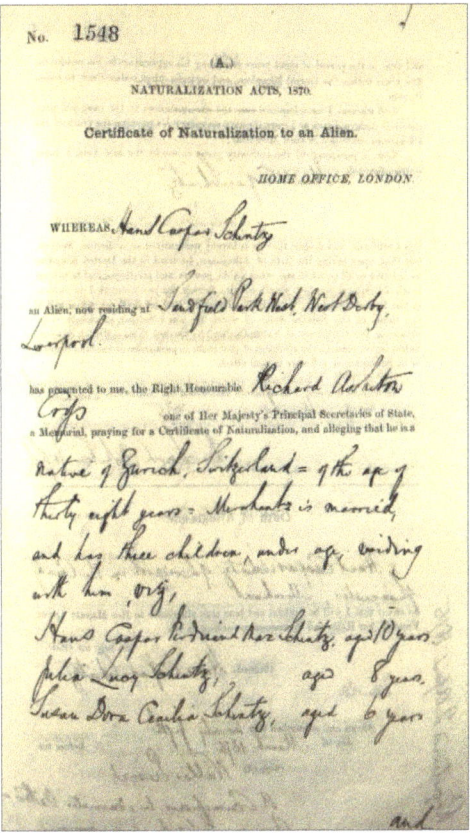 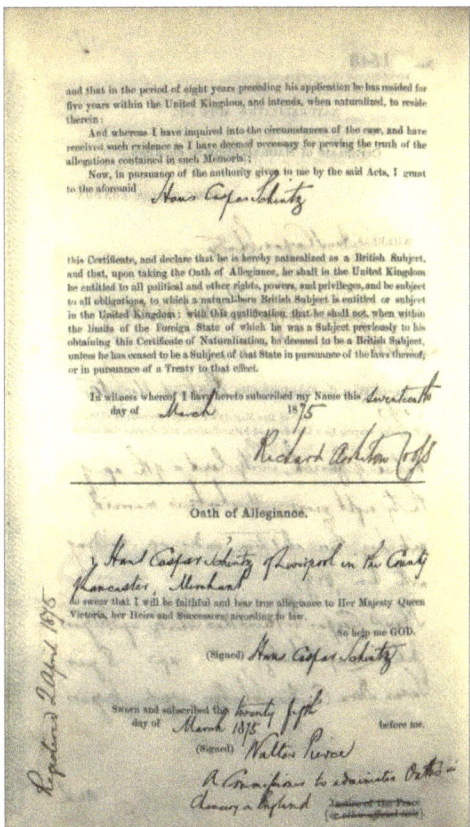

Certificate of Naturalization for Hans Gaspard Schintz dated 25th March 1875.

TNA HO 334/5/1548

Like many of the leading merchants of the time Hans Gaspard was a staunch Unitarian, a creed which encourages business-mindedness and the adherence to high ethical standards. At one time he worshipped at a chapel in Renshaw Street in the Mount Pleasant district of Liverpool but in 1899 the congregation moved to a newly built chapel in Ullet Road, Sefton Park. This was frequented by ship-owning and mercantile families who formed a close network of family and business alliances.

Hans and his wife had three children, all born in Liverpool. The oldest was Julia Lucy (1866 - 1940), who married a surgeon, John Smith Moreton (1856 - 1948), in 1897. They lived at various grand properties around the country including Broadward Hall in Shropshire, Chilworth Manor in Hampshire and finally South Pickenham Hall in Norfolk.

Their second child, Hans Gaspard Ferdinand Max (1865 - 1911), was born the following year and later in life acquired the soubriquet *Mad Max*. He attended Harrow school between 1879 and 1881 and later joined his father as a senior partner in Schintz and Company. He was a member of the Royal Rock Beagle hunt in the Wirral in the 1890s and was also a keen alpine mountaineer. In his application for the Alpine Club in 1888 he listed dozens of climbs which he had made earlier in the decade. From 1886 until 1908 he accompanied the noted Swiss mountaineer, Alois Pollinger, on some of his most hazardous expeditions.[3] On 13 October 1911 he died as a result of a climbing accident near Sargans in Switzerland. His estate was valued at a little over £41,000 and devolved to his father in June 1912 with a further grant of almost £12,000 to William George Wood, his father's accountant, in October that year, after his father's death.

Max with his father, Hans Gaspard Schintz
Robert Freeman

252   ALPINE CLUB REGISTER

1890. With F. L. Littledale, *Aiguilles de Tacul*; *Blaitière*; *Petit Dru*; *Verte*; *Col des Hirondelles*.

1891. *Le Plaret*; *Meije*; *Barre des Écrins* traversed, 10/viii; *Pointe du Vallon des Étages*; *Col de la Lavey*; *Pic d'Olan*, 14/viii (La Montagne, iv. 196; S.T.D. Ann. 1914, p. 116); *Les Bans*, 17/viii; *Gabelhorn* traversed; *Rothorn* traversed.

1892. *Piz Morteratsch* traversed, –/viii (R.M. 1911, pp. 310-11); *Piz Bernina* by the Scharte; *Crast' Agüzza* traversed; *Piz Roseg* traversed; traverse of *Monte Rosso di Scerscen* and *Piz Bernina*; *Grand Cornier* traversed; *Triftjoch*; *Breithorn*, by N. face.

1893. *Castor*; *Pollux*; *Südlenzspitze*; *Nadelhorn*; *Rimpfischhorn* from Adler pass; *Matterhorn* traversed from N. to S., return by *Furggenjoch*; *Dent Blanche* by W. arête (xxiii. 109); *Mominghorn*; *Wellenkuppe* from Triftridge; *Strahlhorn* from Nord End; *Cols d'Hérens* and *de Bertol*.

1894. *Pic Bourcet*; *Le Pavé*; *Pic du Says* (?); *Grande Ruine*, direct from Val d'Étançons; *Meije* traversed, 24/viii; *Râteau* traversed; *Aiguille d'Argentière*.

1895. *Les Périades* traversed; *Aig. des Charmoz* (traverse of all 5 points); *Aig. du Chardonnet*; *Tour Noir*, 1st ascent (there had been a previous descent), 19/viii (xviii. 212, Kurz, 1914 ed., p. 50); *Aig. de Talèfre*; *Aig. de Grépon* (19th ascent), 19/viii; *Mont Mallet*; *Les Droits*.

1896. *Mittag-Egginerhorngrat*; *Weissmies* traversed; *Laquinhorn*; *Portiengrat*; *Monte Leone*.

1899. *Aiguille de Rochefort*, by SE. face, 20/viii (probably 1st ascent from Italian side, R.M. 1900, p. 121; S.A.C.J. xxxv. 297, xxxvi. 263; Kurz, p. 136); *Col des Grandes Jorasses*, 2nd passage (xxvi. 232); *Col Dolent* (C.A.I. Boll. 1901, p. 95); Signor Bobba, in mentioning the last expedition, describes Schintz as 'un Alpinista che lascia traccia delle sue numerose e difficile imprese—lo constituamo deplorandolo—soltanto sui libelli delle guide e—sulle cime'. The lists given above up to 1896 are preserved in Aloys Pollinger's book and probably nowhere else. Very little is traceable of his doings in later years.

British Isles. See G. A. Solly, 1891 and 93.

Extract from the Alpine Club registers showing Max Schintz's exploits between 1890 and 1899

Alpine Club

Max's ashes are housed in the columbarium at Anfield Cemetery, Liverpool in a niche fronted by a white stone plaque which reads *In memory of Hans Ferdinand Max Gaspard Schintz, born January 20th 1865, died October 13th 1911*.[4]

The third of Hans Gaspard and Anna's children is the subject of this account. Susan Dora Cecilia (known usually as Dora) was born in Liverpool on 7th October 1868.

Birth certificate of Dora Schintz

Most of Hans Gaspard's wealth came from saltpetre nitrates sourced in Tarapaca province, northern Chile, raw materials that were used in the production of fertiliser and explosives. The Chilean nitrate business was dominated by the British from the early 1890s and at the peak of nitrate production twenty years later there were 36 such companies. Hans Schintz was a director of or a shareholder in several of these companies including the New Tamarugal Nitrates Co., the San Sebastian Nitrate Co. and the San Lorenzo Nitrate Company. His success in this industry resulted in his soubriquet *The Nitrate King*.

Another South American connection was through the Helvetia Land Company which Hans Gaspard set up in 1906 along with his son, Max, and another merchant, William Henry Hasler. The company purchased a ranch called Estancia El Descado[5] near Buenos Aires in Argentina. This comprised about 16,000 acres of land together with established herds of cattle.

Certificate of Incorporation of the Helvetica Land Company, 1906.
TNA BT 31/17777/89002

In about 1890 Hans Gaspard acquired a fertiliser business in Auby, a village in France about 30 miles from Lille. Here he traded as Schintz et Fils, a company which in 1911 became the Société de Produits Chimiques et Engrais d'Auby (the Auby Company). This was a very substantial enterprise with an extensive factory which occupied an area of some 42 acres between the Deule canal and the Paris to Lille railway line. At the very beginning he recruited a Polish chemist, Casimir Gasiorowski as factory manager through whose efforts the company became extremely successful. Casimir became mayor of Auby in 1904, a position he held until 1919.

The Auby factory in 1930.
From a postcard.

In 1906, through an Indenture of Settlement, Hans Gaspard gifted each of his three children in trust one third of his 90% holding in the company, and in addition one third of approximately £180,000. After Max died in 1911, his share was split between Dora and her sister, Julia, giving them a fund of £90,000 each.

Hans Gaspard's sister, Anna Susannah, married Georg Melchior Burkly. Their son, Leonard Georg Burkly, also a merchant, is known to have travelled on business with Hans Gaspard to Chile in the 1890s. Leonard's wife, Beatrice, and daughter, Betty, became Dora's life-long friends.

Hans Gaspard was reputedly the owner of the finest team of horses and carriages in Liverpool. He is known to have attended a stud sale in Highgate, London at which he purchased two horses, Metal and Magnet, for 440 guineas. Dora's mother had a Brougham (a light, four-wheeled horse-drawn carriage), a Victoria (similar to a Brougham but with the addition of a coachman's box-seat) and employed a coachman.

During the 1880s and 1890s his name (and that of his gardener, Mr Heaney) frequently appeared in the local press as an exhibitor of prize chrysanthemums, and while living in Sefton Park, Liverpool, he made part of his land available for the local amateur gardeners' association.

Hans Gaspard is known to have travelled to Switzerland on vacation and appears to have maintained a property there called Grabengarten at 43 Bahnhofstrasse in Zurich. This was probably built by his 3x great grandfather, also Hans Gaspard (1697–1766), but was demolished in 1914 and the Munzhof (the mint) built in its place.

Grabengarten, the house on Bahnhoffstrasse, Zurich belonging to Hans Schintz in 1912.

Public domain

EARLY LIFE IN LIVERPOOL

Despite extensive research of all available documents, and interviews with members of her family, it has not been possible to discover much about Dora's early life other than she lived with her parents at a number of different addresses in well-to-do areas in Liverpool. Districts to the southeast of Liverpool City centre were mercantile enclaves inhabited by some of Britain's richest men. By 1870 the family was living at St Clare, Sandfield Park, West Derby, but by 1881 had moved to Sefton Park, Toxteth. From 1884 to 1894 they lived at Mossley House, Mossley Hill. This beautiful ivy-covered building, in so-called 'cathedral' architectural style was one of the finest residences in Liverpool, later converted into hospital accommodation. Finally, from 1894 to 1922, the family moved to Childwall Hall. All of these properties appear to have been leased and not owned by the family.

By her early twenties Dora had become well-known in social circles, attending balls given by the Mayor of Liverpool in January 1891 and 1892 and the Athole Highland Gathering, Dundee in September 1891. She was also present at the Liverpool Polo club pony show in June 1894 and fashionable garden parties in July 1894 and August 1899.

Dora was involved with numerous charitable organisations in Liverpool. In 1895 she attended a pageant at Otterspool House in the Algburth district of Liverpool in aid of the Liverpool Association for the Care and Protection of Young Girls. In the same year she and her mother were present at the opening of a bazaar in St George's Hall, Liverpool (one of the finest neo-classical buildings in the world) on behalf of the Church of England Society for Providing Homes for Waifs and Strays. The latter event appears to have been more of a social gathering as *The Gentlewoman* of April 25 devoted several column inches to a detailed description of the ladies' attire. Dora and her mother were described as follows: '*Mrs Schintz appeared in green satin with berthe* (a trim added to the neckline of a dress) *of beautiful lace, and Miss Schintz, heliotrope with chiffon bodice to match*'.[6]

Both her parents gave generously to charity and Dora seems to have been particularly keen to support voluntary hospitals. By her own admission later in life, she never spent much money on herself, most of her clothes being made by her maid or herself, and she ate frugally.

Mossley House in 1910

U.S. National Library of Medicine

CHILDWALL HALL

Childwall Hall was Dora's family home for almost 30 years. It was designed by the famous architect John Nash and built for Bamber Gascoyne in 1780 to replace an earlier manor house. Ownership of the Hall passed through marriage to the 2nd Marquess of Salisbury and from 1821 it was leased to a number of tenants including Ralph Brocklebank, a Liverpool Merchant and co-director of the San Lorenzo Nitrate Co. with Hans Schintz, and from 1894 to 1922 by Hans himself and his family who were the last residents. Thereafter it served as a clubhouse of the Childwall Golf Club until 1938. Liverpool Corporation purchased 50 acres of land in 1939 and was later given the Hall as a gift by the 5th Marquess. It was intended to establish a college here but the building was found to be in poor condition and was demolished in 1949. However, remnants of the ornamental gardens, carriage drive and stable block remain. The history of Childwall Hall has been well-documented in History of Childwall by Jonathon Wild[7].

At Childwall Hall the Schintz family had up to 16 indoor servants. By July 1900 Dora seems to have taken over the day-to-day running of the household as it was she rather than her mother who placed a newspaper advertisement for a maid. Her requirements were quite specific:

> 'Wanted, Useful MAID; thoroughly experienced dressmaker, neat sewer, good cut and careful fitting essential; not under 5'4"; no fringe; quiet place, no travelling, 10 servants; dogs; excellent and long references required; wages £28, all found – Miss Schintz, Childwall Hall, near Liverpool'.[8]

CHILDWALL HALL | 25

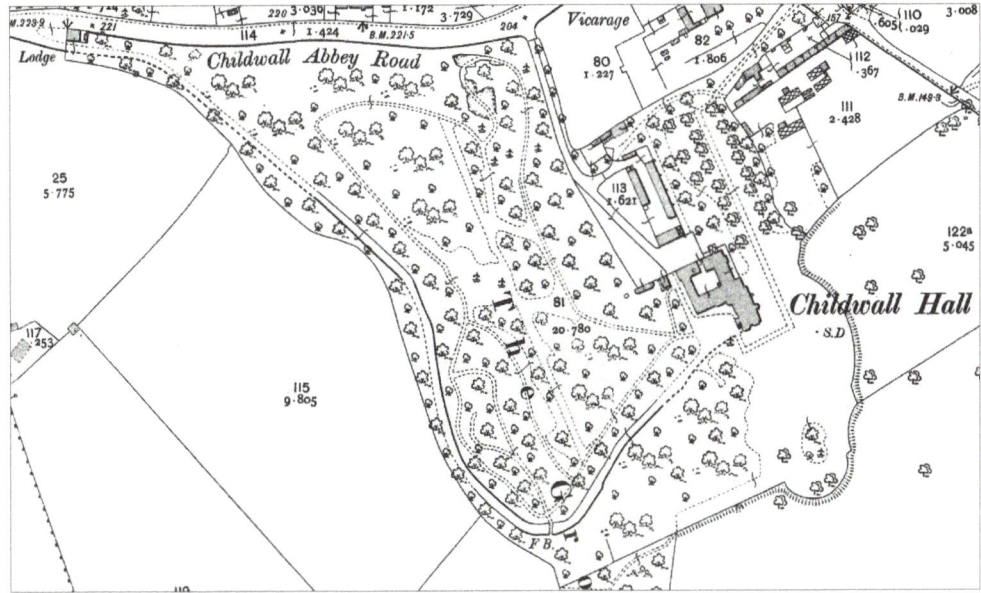

Map of Childwall Hall estate (1904) showing the
hall and extensive stables to the northeast.
Public domain.

Colourised photograph of Childwall Hall
taken by Dora Schintz (early 1900s)
TNA COPY1/502/149

The Schintz family owned several dogs. Among them was a Great Dane named Tyras which was buried in Childwall Wood. Its headstone, which was engraved *In memory of Tyras the Great Dane, born July 1895, died December 1904*, survived until recently.

The stables at Childwall Hall at the turn of the century with possibly Tyras the Great Dane (above) and the entrance to the stables (right).

Annabel Collenette

The stables at Childwall were extensive and well-appointed. They would have provided Dora with the opportunity to develop her interest in hackney horses which was to become a large part of her life before the First World War and remained a life-long passion. There are no photographs of Hans or Dora with a horse, but an image of Dora's sister at Mossley House shows an example of a magnificent carriage and harness.

While living with her parents at Childwall Hall Dora appears to have tried her hand at photography as there are four excellent views of the Hall and grounds taken by her. She registered the photographs for copyright in October 1906 with the intention of publishing them as postcards. Two examples have been colourised to great effect and are shown here.

Colourised photograph of one of the Schintz horses outside Mossley House with Dora's sister Julia Lucy driving a two-wheeled gig (before 1894). The coachman is probably Joseph Morris.

Annabel Collenette

Aerial view of the stables at Childwall Hall 1932

britainfromabove.org, EPW037684

**Colourised photograph of Childwall Hall in the
snow taken by Dora Schintz (early 1900s)**
TNA COPY1/502/396

Dora first came to the attention of the press when she made a remarkably sudden entry into the world of hackney horse competitions. She is known to have started acquiring good bloodstock from other prominent hackney owners and breeders by 1905 while she was still living at Childwall Hall. She was elected a life member of the Hackney Horse Society in February 1906, and the records of that organisation show that she continued to build up a large stable of prize-winning horses over the next few years. These included Manilla, Morocco, Martello and Mogador which were all well-known show horses by 1907. It was in this year that she made a name for herself at the first International Horse Show at the Olympia Stadium in London where her Countess Clio won first prize. Morocco, Mogador, Martello, Catalina and later, Aerial Queen and Woodhatch Ruth, were all frequent winners of many coveted prizes at Olympia and other shows up and down the country. Shortly after the Olympia show, the magazine *Horses Illustrated* printed an extensive article entitled *Miss Dora Schintz's Hackney and Harness Stud*. In this article reference is made to her having owned hackneys '*for some years but has, we believe, never shown them before, with the exception of Morocco at Prescot in May*'.[9] One of her first horses was Knowle Belinda which featured in Sir Humphrey Trafford's *Horses of the British Empire* published in 1907.[10]

A photograph from Dora's family album, date and location unknown. It is tempting to think this is Dora with one of her hackneys.
Annabel Collenette

Knowle Belinda, one of Dora's first horses
Horses of the British Empire

THICKTHORN

Thickthorn in recent years, now Kenilworth Manor Nursing Home
Kenilworth Manor Nursing Home

Perhaps in anticipation of Dora's success at Olympia, in March 1907 her father acquired an estate at Thickthorn near Kenilworth, Warwickshire from lawyer Richard Rideout Beard, county High Sheriff. This purchase was made specifically to provide Dora with the opportunity to breed and train hackney horses. In November that year her mother acquired some adjoining plots of land (32 acres at Station Farm and Ashfield). All this land eventually was transferred to Dora by deeds of gift in 1908 and 1912. In 1910, Dora purchased a couple of small plots herself increasing the total area of her estate to about 211 acres. The house was a substantial early 19th century stone mansion with five reception rooms and 13 bedrooms, dressing rooms and bathrooms. More importantly there were also extensive stabling facilities. In addition to the main house and grounds, there was a lodge house and several cottages, small holdings and a farm. One residence on the estate called Woodlands was often used by patients from the Liverpool Home for Incurables.

An aerial view of Thickthorn House and stables in 1969.
© Historic England Archive. Aerofilms Collection EAW194849

Almost immediately after the purchase, plans went ahead for a new stable block, stud farm and exercise yard. The stable block was enclosed by a 20-foot-high castellated wall to match the style of the house. It had stables for 10 horses and a garage for six cars. The stud farm foaling stables had a centre aisle, 7 boxes, 2 foaling boxes, a saddle room and covered and open yards while the roof was surmounted by a clock tower. Alongside was an exercise circuit which was accessed by a track leading from the stables. There was also a stud groom's house and lodge. The £60,000 cost of this extraordinary building and other improvements on the estate was borne by her parents.

At the same time, it was reported in the press that a *'complete blotting out of the landscape taking place with hundreds of yards of close, blank, unornamented high fencing being erected enclosing the whole of the Thickthorn estate'.*[11] It transpired that the fence which varied in height from 6 to 9 feet was erected to keep the local hunt horses away from Dora's brood mares.

Colourised photograph of the entrance to the Thickthorn stable block.
Robin Leach

The building of the stables did not go without a hitch. In early 1910 an architect, Mr Gibb, employed by Dora to oversee drawings and specifications and to advise her on the work being conducted, sued her in The High Court for £190 in unpaid fees. However, she claimed that he had been negligent and had allowed poor workmanship to be carried out and made a counter claim for £2304 6s. 3d. Among the problems was mortar which was of very poor quality. It was finally judged that a great part of the work had been *'executed in a most disgraceful way'*[12] and Dora was awarded £500 compensation plus costs by the Official Referee.

In 1912 an extension to the stable block was made to house a kind of internal combustion engine, a dynamo and battery store. This was to supply the stables and possibly the house as well with electricity.

Some of Dora's employees were housed on the estate. The 1911 census records grooms Charles Dear and Michael Melerangi at the Thickthorn stables, stud-groom Frederick Edwards and his family at Thickthorn stud farm. Domestic groom, Alfred Taylor, gardener William Stevens and woodman Henry Mills were all accommodated in other buildings on the estate.

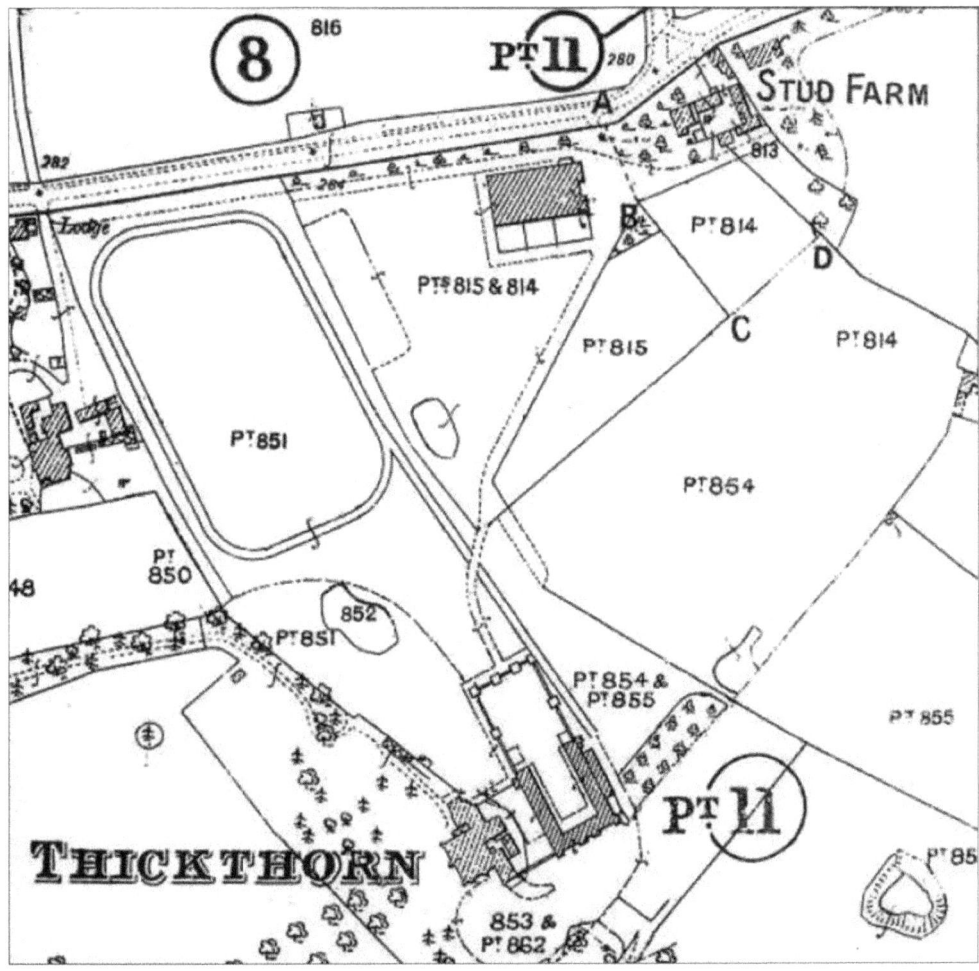

Map of Thickthorn from 1922 sale catalog showing the stud farm, the exercise circuit and the adjacent foaling stables.

Warwickshire County Record Office, EAC 631

The acquisition of a stud farm enabled Dora to start breeding from her own bloodstock. The first was Bronze Belinda, which foaled in 1907. Reflecting her favourite hackney colour, a rich mahogany shade of chestnut, *Bronze* was the registered prefix chosen by Dora for horses foaled at the Thickthorn stud. Interestingly, among the family heirlooms is a pair of hackneys cast in bronze on a plinth.

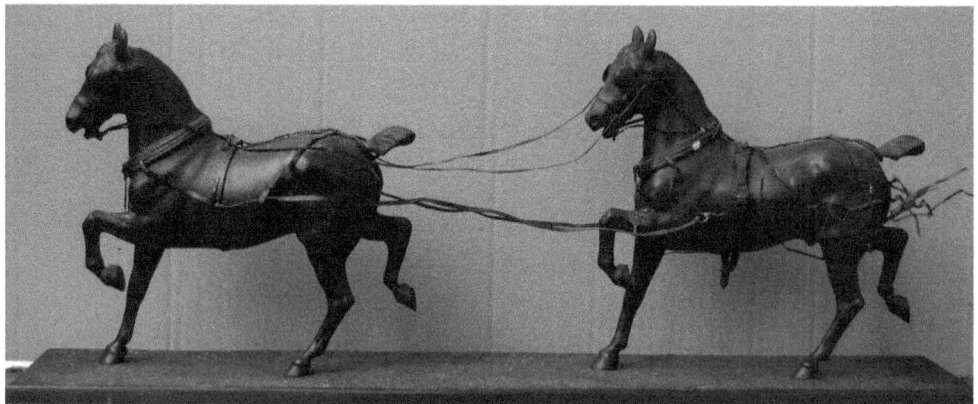

A pair of hackneys in bronze belonging to Dora Schintz.
Annabel Collenette

It was usual practice for horses entering hackney events to undergo a veterinary inspection. A newspaper report revealed that at the Birmingham show in June 1911 Dora's hackney mare, Catalina, won an event which would entitle her to a silver medal, subject to being certified free from hereditary disease by a Hackney Horse Society's appointed veterinary surgeon.[13] Unfortunately, the vet appointed on that occasion did not pass Catalina for an undisclosed reason. Dora contended that in consequence the mare had depreciated greatly in value and at the Birmingham Assize in March 1912 she sued the vet for damages. Her case was supported by a number of other veterinary surgeons who were called to bear witness. It appears that no compromise could be reached, and the judgment was awarded to the defendant with costs. Whether an appeal was made is not known but over the next few years Catalina went on to win a string of awards at many prestigious events around the country.

Dora was a very shrewd judge of hackneys, always purchasing the highest quality horses. Money would appear to have been no problem as she paid the asking price for any horse she wished to acquire. Her policy was to possess only the very best animals that money could buy. In 1910 she paid 270 guineas, equivalent to about £25,000 at today's prices, for one of her prize winners, Woodhatch Ruth, when she was an unbroken three-year-old, and that was considered to have been a bargain.

At the beginning of the 1900s, British hackneys were being exported all over the world. Dora seems to have been involved in this international trade from the start, as during 1906 she sold a hackney called Tarantella to an American in New York and in 1909 she received a good price for a horse from a buyer in Crewe.

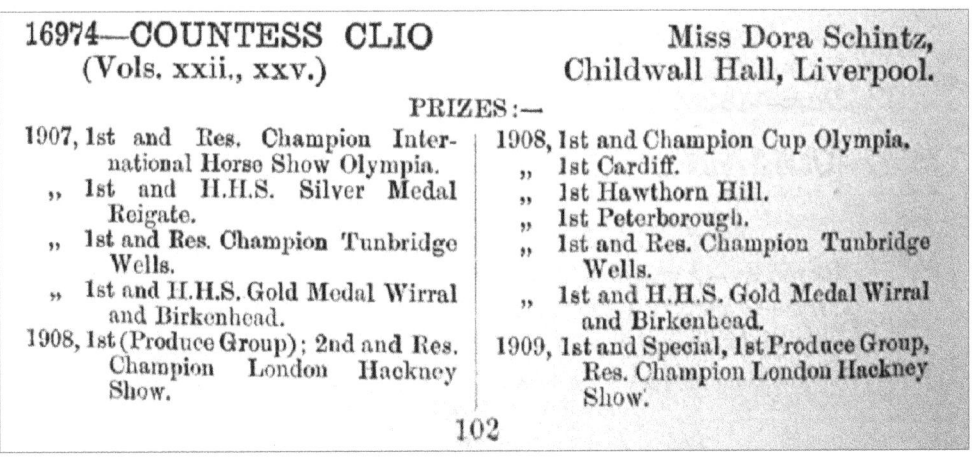

Extract from Hackney Horse Society stud book showing prizes won by just one of Dora's horses, Countess Clio, in two years[14].

In 1913 she had fifteen show horses registered with the Hackney Horse Society and she maintained a stable that included some of the finest examples in the country. The breeding and showing of hackneys was largely a male preserve at this time and there was only a handful of women breeders. One of these was the coaching legend Sylvia Brocklebank, against whom Dora competed in many shows and with whom she was no doubt acquainted through their fathers' business connections in Liverpool.

The foaling stables at Thickthorn. Part of the high fence can just be seen to the left.

Warwickshire County Record Office, EAC631

A 1922 view of the inside of the stud farm showing the stables at the side and a car outside the coach house.

Warwickshire County Record Office, EAC631

Dora resided at Thickthorn for only about three months of the year, the rest of the time being spent at Childwall with her parents. Sometimes, however, her parents would visit her at Thickthorn. On one of these occasions things did not go to plan. According to the local press on 15 August 1908[15] she sent a one-horse brougham to meet her parents at the railway station. As soon as they were seated the horse bolted sending one of the shafts through the carriage. The startled creature then galloped down the road and the carriage overturned, demolished a gatepost and was badly damaged. Mrs Schintz received a wound to the forehead which was stitched by a local doctor. She was later taken to Thickthorn where she received further treatment. The coachman was severely bruised and the horse had severe cuts which were attended to by the stud groom.

Dora's hackneys, Catalina and Woodhatch Ruth, with a spider phaeton being driven by George Bond.

British Library 7291.i.24

As well as participating in local shows, Dora travelled the length and breadth of England to exhibit her horses. Attending these events was a feat in itself as at this time the only available means of transport was a train to the nearest station and then driving the horses the remaining distance to the venue. In Sylvia Brocklebank's contemporary autobiographical account *The Road and the Ring*, she recalls that '*the horses left Liverpool by train for Kingston-on-Thames where they were to be stabled before going on to Olympia*'.[16] At this time it was common practice for horse boxes to be attached to scheduled trains. They were typically laid out to accommodate a number of horses and a groom, and there was also storage space for hay. Carriages were loaded onto flat wagons.

Dora was well known in the hackney horse community and articles about her and her horses appear *inter alia* in Geoffrey Bennett's *Famous Harness Horses*.[17] There are accounts of Dora herself driving a four in hand at the Birkenhead Agricultural Society show and with three horses abreast in the vicinity of Thickthorn, but her head groom, George Bond, drove them to nearly all their later victories. It was not only the horses that were the finest money could buy but also the harnesses which were alleged to have been adorned with gold and bore the Schintz family crest.

Harness with the Schintz family crest.
Annabel Collenette

It must have been wonderful to see these beautifully turned-out horses being put through their paces. A newspaper contributor in 1937 reminisced that '*It was one of the sights of the shows to see Miss Schintz drive a magnif-*

icent four-in-hand into the huge arena. Her horses were always in beautiful condition and with them she won many coveted prizes.[18] A local resident recalled seeing '*her high stepping ponies pulling her two-wheel gig, two ponies running in tandem looking beautiful with their feet hardly touching the ground*'.

Not only did Dora secure many championship prizes for her own horses, but she also awarded prizes to other contestants in the form of cups and cash. In 1913 at Olympia she gave prizes for the smartest fire brigade horses and for driving.

Dora continued to breed and show hackneys until the outbreak of the First World War after which her horses were not shown again and she disappeared from the hackney scene as quickly as she had appeared on it.

As well as being noted for her horses Dora was also renowned locally for her generosity. For example, she is recorded as donating £20 to the Leamington Institute 1911. The pupils of St John's School, Kenilworth were also the recipients of much kindness. As a local newspaper records:

> '*There is no-one in Kenilworth who does as much in the way of surreptitious charity as Miss Schintz. Ever since taking up residency in Kenilworth it has been her practice at Christmas to bring wonderful cheer to the hearts of the whole of the children attending the St John's schools, but no public acknowledgement has been made and Miss Schintz has kept out of the limelight in this as in many other generous action*'.[19]

In her generosity towards these children, in 1913 she gave a mint half-crown to every child and a selection of gifts including watches, knives, workboxes, knitted garments, scarves and crackers. The following Christmas she laid on a party for the 200 pupils and provided presents individually addressed to each child. Even the four who were absent through illness received their presents as well as party food. Such parties appear to have been hosted not by Miss Schintz herself but by her employees. In 1916 this was the responsibility of George Rose, her estate agent, and his wife.

During the war some of her staff were called up. However, a number of them were excused for various reasons and their names appeared in the press at the time. These included Alfred Taylor who was stud groom and Charles

Dear his assistant, and George Rose. One wonders what influence Dora might have brought to bear on the examining committee.

In another act of generosity, in 1917 Dora provided three acres of her land to create 24 allotments for local residents.

As part of Kenilworth's celebrations to mark the end of the war, on 20 July 1919 Dora held a party for fifty of her Thickthorn employees. There were sports and games, tea was provided and the event ended with a firework display.

After the war there was a housing shortage locally and the Kenilworth Urban District Council tried to persuade Dora to move three of her staff families from their cottages on the estate to Woodlands so as to make the vacated properties available for other people. She claimed that only part of this house was habitable and that the other part was already occupied by her groom, who had returned disabled from the war, and his family. At a council meeting in June 1920 through her estate agent, George Rose, she forcefully declined to allow people not in her service to move in and threatened legal action if the council persisted in their demands.

Like her father, she also took part in less prestigious competitions at local shows. In August 1908, a model village designed by her won the County Cup at the Leamington flower show and later attracted much interest at the Kenilworth show.

In March 1915, her chauffeur at Thickthorn, Norman Molesworth Dunkley, came to the attention of the press when he appeared at the Warwickshire Quarter Sessions in Coventry for dangerous driving, a charge which he denied. The case was eventually dismissed after Dora's footman, Joseph Wright, corroborated Dunkley's account. Dunkley was later to be involved in a much more serious incident.

The first indication that Dora wished to sell Thickthorn was seen in an advanced notice of an auction in November 1921. This was shortly after she had purchased Ottershaw Park and the death of her mother. At this point only about half the estate (107 acres) was advertised for sale, but by the time of the auction on 29 March 1922 at The Regent Hotel in Leamington all 211 acres were on the market in 18 lots.

BY DIRECTION OF MISS DORA C. SCHINTZ

WARWICKSHIRE,

In the centre of a fine Hunting Country,
One mile from Kenilworth and three and a half miles from Leamington.

THE FREEHOLD RESIDENTIAL ESTATE
known as

THICKTHORN,

including the
SUBSTANTIAL STONE MANSION HOUSE in the Tudor style of architecture, occupying a delightful position, about 300 feet above sea level—in the centre of an undulating well-timbered Park, and containing halls, five reception rooms, 13 bed, dressing, and bath rooms.
COMPLETE MODERN STABLING, with accommodation for 10 horses, garage for six. Exercise yard.

THE STUD BUILDING,
a well-planned erection with clock tower, comprising nine boxes, &c., with covered and open yards. Stud groom's house, &c. Lodge.
Electric Light. Company's Water and Gas. Telephone.
Matured old grounds. Park lands.

TWO MEDIUM-SIZED HOUSES.
THE LODGE AND WOODLANDS,
with grounds of 3 and 12 acres respectively.

STUD FARM.
Small holdings. Accommodation Lands and Cottages, the whole extending to about

211 ACRES.

HUNTING AND GOLF.
VACANT POSSESSION
on Completion of the Principal Lots.
To be offered for SALE by AUCTION, as a whole, in Blocks, or in 18 Lots, at LEAMINGTON SPA, in March (unless previously sold privately).

Solicitors :—Messrs. GODFREY WARR and Co., 85, Gracechurch-street, E.C.3.

Auctioneers :—Messrs. KNIGHT, FRANK and RUTLEY, 20, Hanover-square, W.1.

Announcement of Thickthorn estate sale.

The Observer, 27 November 1921

The sale was not a success and only one small lot sold. Thickthorn House and the stud farm received no bids, other lots such as Kenilworth Lodge and Woodlands failed to reach their reserves and 197 acres remained unsold. In May that year the estate was mortgaged for £56,000[20] and in May 1923 for another £10400 and in 1924 for a further £18,000. A sale of furniture took place in October 1922 and the house found a buyer in 1926 having stood empty for two years. Other parts of the estate were gradually sold off piecemeal. Dora's interest in Thickthorn lasted until November, 1930 when the remaining 130 acres, including what was listed as *'the famous stud farm',*[21] were sold at auction for £13,800. The house was restored in 1987 to become Kenilworth Manor nursing home and is now a Grade II listed building while the estate has been divided up.

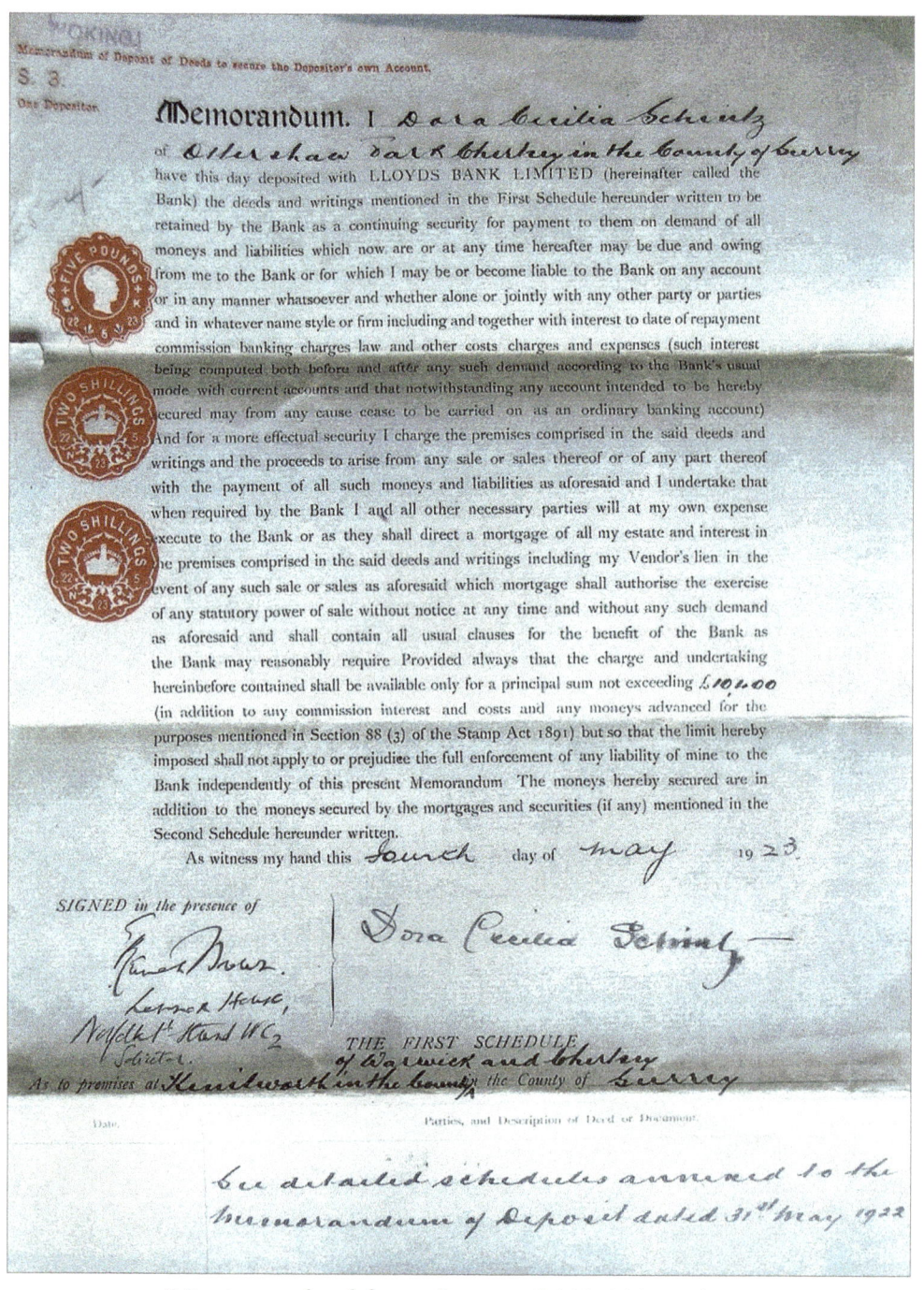

Mortgage deed for a charge of £10,400 against Dora's Thickthorn estate dated 4 May 1923.

Plan of the Thickthorn estate showing the various lots for sale by auction in 1922.
Warwickshire County Record Office, EAC 631

DEATH OF HANS GASPARD

In the midst of her hackney successes in the pre-war period on 5 August 1912 Dora's father Hans Gaspard died. He had been ill for some time with lung problems and finally succumbed to pneumonia. His funeral at Anfield Crematorium in Liverpool was a grand affair and attended by Dora and her brother-in-law, John Moreton, Childwall Hall servants, local dignitaries and the Swiss Consul. Thickthorn servants sent floral tributes. His ashes are preserved in the Anfield cemetery columbarium in a niche next to his son, Max.[22] A white stone plaque reads '*In memory of Hans Gaspard Schintz, born March 19th 1837, died August 5th 1912*.'

From his English estate he provided generously for his wife, children, grandchildren, nephews and employees. He left a life interest of £150,000 in trust for Dora and Julia, as well as a gift of £100,000 (equivalent to £8-10 million today) to Dora, which was added to the 1906 settlement fund. Dora also inherited her father's interest in the Helvetia Land Co. Ltd and a stake in the Auby Company as well as portraits of his ancestors. The residue of his estate was distributed in equal shares between Dora and Julia. The value of this residue is

Plaque recording Hans Gaspard Schintz in the columbarium at Anfield cemetery.

Jonathon Wild

difficult determine such is the complexity of his will. At this point Dora had become a fabulously wealthy woman.

Hans's two grandchildren received £50,000 jointly in trust, and each of his nephews received £1000. He also provided £3500 to Casimir Gasiorowski, manager of the Auby Company, £3000 to his cashier (Asa John Thomas), £500 to his bookkeeper (William George Wood), £300 to his coachman (Charles Scafe), £200 to his head housemaid (Sarah Bellamy) and £500 to his gardener in Zurich (Robert Schuttanner). He also directed that two years' wages should be given to each business employee with 5 years or more service, and he bequeathed generous sums to all the servants in his employment. He made no specific bequests to charity but instructed his wife to make donations totalling £20,000. She chose the Country Hospital for Children, Home for Incurables, Royal Southern Hospital, Hospital for Women, Liverpool Royal Infirmary, Bluecoat Hospital, and the Liverpool Seamen's Orphanage.

His English will, which ran to twenty-two pages, contained a clause disinheriting any child or remoter issue who became a Catholic or married a Catholic. He declared, furthermore, that anyone having an interest in his will who disputed its conditions would forfeit their benefits. Judging from this, his Unitarian beliefs were undoubtedly very strongly held.[23]

In addition, the value of his real estate in Switzerland was undisclosed and was dealt with separately, according to Swiss law. His last known Swiss will was deposited at the notary's office of the Zurich Altstadt on 2 November 1887, but unfortunately the testimony itself could not be found so it is not possible to know what assets, other than his house in Zurich, were in his possession and who benefitted from his bequests.

As a result of her inheritance, Dora had become wealthy in her own right, unusual for an Edwardian woman. Being in her own words '*addicted to charity*', the income from the trust set up under the terms of her inheritance enabled her to spend freely on charitable works. She was personally involved with the Liverpool Home for Incurables before the First World War and she continued to give them support.

Despite her great wealth she spent little of her vast fortune on herself. A friend commented to the press that '*She spent right and left, but always for the good of others.*'[49]

FIRST WORLD WAR AND ARROWE HALL

Dora had just come into her fortune when war broke out and she straightaway proceeded to spend large sums of money alleviating the sufferings of those affected. In published subscription lists she usually ranked amongst the most generous of subscribers. For example, she donated £2000 to the National Relief Fund in August 1914, £1000 to the French Red Cross in 1915, £150 to Transport of the wounded in August 1916 and £100 to France's Day Fund in 1917. Many hundreds of wounded soldiers owed her a deep debt of gratitude for what she did for them.

The first ever motorised ambulances to transport the wounded were used in the First World War. Faced with unprecedented numbers of casualties in September 1914, an appeal was made by the Red Cross for donations of private vehicles for use as ambulances. Presumably in response to this, the following month Dora provided a four-stretcher ambulance for use in France where it saw service in various theatres of war including Béthune, La Base, Ypres and Neuve Chapelle.[24] It was built on a Sheffield Simplex chassis, likely to have been from one of the Schintz family cars.

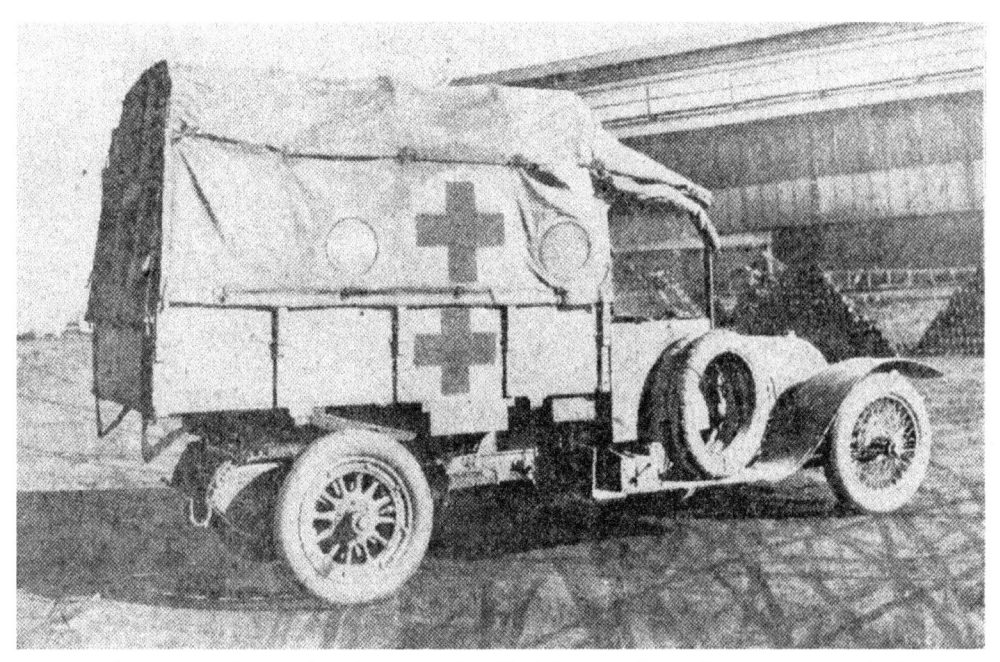

The ambulance built on a Sheffield Simplex chassis provided by Dora for the war effort in 1914. Seen here on its return to the Sheffield works for an overhaul in April 1915.

Sheffield Daily Telegraph 15 Apr 1915

At the beginning of the war, Colonel McCalmont, the owner of the Arrowe Hall estate in Woodchurch near Birkenhead, offered his house to the War Office for use as an auxiliary military hospital. Entirely at her own expense Dora equipped it, including an operating theatre, at the cost of £30,000. She also paid the salaries of a team of doctors and trained nurses and funded its upkeep. In addition, she supplied a fleet of ambulances and her own Rolls Royce cars to transfer patients between the station and the Hall. Dora later claimed that cheques sent by the War Office for the running costs of the hospital were always torn up[25]. She also claimed that the offer of an OBE in recognition of her services had been declined,[52] but no evidence has come to light that this was the case. She was, however, honoured for valuable nursing services rendered in connection with the war effort by having her name brought to the attention of the Secretary of State for War.[26]

Arrowe Hall in the 1920s.
From a postcard

When the hospital first opened there were beds for fifty wounded soldiers but this number later grew to between two and three hundred. The beautiful 1000-acre estate was certainly an agreeable place for rehabilitating injured soldiers. Dora took on the role of Commandant. The Matron was Miss Grace Morgan who in 1918 received the Royal Red Cross (2nd Class) for her services to nursing.[27] Medical staff receiving particular mention for providing valuable nursing services in 1918 included Sister J Nicholls and Sister E Park.

The success of the hospital depended not only on paid staff but on volunteers, some of whom can be identified in British Red Cross records. Mr Hurley gave his service as a hairdresser every Sunday throughout the war. He also raised considerable amounts of money for charities and was a supplier of '*smokes*', a service which was most appreciated by the patients. Mr Smith was a VAD Quartermaster[28] who organised the distribution of patients on arrival, took soldiers to theatre, drove an ambulance and lent his own car for use by the British Red Cross Society. He also organised numerous social events such as concert parties, whist drives and sports for the patients. Another member of staff was Miss Cowan who provided her services as a VAD masseuse.

In 1917, the estate was sold to Lord Leverhulme who allowed its use as a hospital to continue for the duration of the war. The time spent on her activities at Arrowe Hall and her involvement with other charitable works may explain why Dora gave up competing with her hackneys.

An amusing event occurred during one of her charity fundraising efforts in Liverpool during October 1916 when she was reported in the Liverpool Echo to have been assisted by her pet monkey, Jacko, in enticing people to contribute:

> 'Miss Dora Schintz who made a tour of Liverpool in her car selling flags for charity caused great amusement by entering the Cotton Exchange with her monkey, now the mascot of her hospital at Arrowe Hall. Members who already wore flags were forced to buy another while one old gentleman who a few minutes earlier had openly declared his firm intention of not buying a flag because of his prejudice to the Government relying on charity, unable to resist the appeal, presented Jacko with half-a-crown. A few minutes later on entering the reading room he was again tackled by Jacko and his mistress and bought another flag.'[29]

A serious episode with repercussions for Arrowe Hall was reported on February 27 1915, when Dora was the defendant in a court case heard at Chester Assizes.[30] This concerned an incident on 20 December 1913 in which her car, driven by her chauffeur Norman Dunkley, was in collision with a pedestrian on the road at Backford near Chester. As a result of the accident, the pedestrian, Frederick Woods, was rendered unconscious and received serious injuries to his head, spine and limbs and spent 6 months in Chester Infirmary. He stated later that he had been maimed for life and, as a consequence, was unable to follow his occupation as a groom. He accused the chauffeur of negligence, claiming that he had been driving recklessly and that he had not sounded his horn as a warning. Woods issued a claim for damages of £1500 plus further costs for the special care he had required since his discharge from hospital. Dora was of the opinion that the accident was Wood's fault entirely as he had stepped in front of the car. Nevertheless, she offered an *ex gratia* payment of £250. According to one account she also offered to put Woods under her care. However, the jury found in the plaintiff's favour and the judge ordered Dora to pay £650 in damages plus costs.

Arrowe Hall during The First World War. Dora Schintz (centre) with patients and hospital staff.

Annabel Collenette

Enlargement of part of the previous image showing Dora Schintz (centre) with patients and staff.

Dora was so incensed by what she believed to be a miscarriage of justice that she wrote to the Liverpool Echo on 11 March implying that the injured man's condition had been made worse by the police insisting he was bundled into a passing car rather than waiting for an ambulance to take him to hospital.[31] She went on to say that to mark her sense of the *'gross wrong involved in the verdict'* she had closed Arrowe Park hospital. She claimed that arrangements were already in place to transfer the injured soldiers to the Fazakerley Military Hospital in Liverpool. It seems that Dora carried out her threat as on 16 March 1915, a local newspaper reported that wounded soldiers had been moved from Arrowe Hall to Rhyl Convalescent Home.[32] An editorial in the press at the time asked her to reconsider.[33] Whether or not it was this article alone that brought about a change of heart is not known but it appears that she reopened the hospital in April and according to her own later account, she ran it until 1919.

She also used Woodlands on her Thickthorn estate as a summer holiday retreat for patients from the Liverpool Home for Incurables with which she was actively involved. Groups of six to twelve patients at a time were accommodated for periods of between five and nine weeks, each group being accompanied by a nurse from Arrowe Park hospital. In the Miscellaneous Donations section of the 1912 annual report of the Home she is recorded as having provided *'Holiday expenses of patients to Kenilworth, drives, game, rabbits, vegetables, fruit, wine, jelly, chicken dinner, garden party, new garments, flowers every week, stout daily for a patient.'*[34]

From 1917 to 1922 Dora financed the Schintz Nursing Home for Incurables at 31 Greenheys Road in Toxteth providing every comfort for the inmates. The home was decorated in pink and white and staffed by nurses, one of whom had been at Arrowe Hall. She is said to have spent many thousands of pounds in this way. Advertisements for staff in the local papers in June and July 1918 read *'Cook (good, plain) wages £30 and uniform…..', 'Housemaid…. good refs essential',* and *'Kitchenmaid: wages £18-20 and uniform'*.[35]

31 Greenheys Road in c.2023 once the Schintz Nursing Home for Incurables.

Besides looking after the needs of the wounded and incurables, Dora often helped to set them up in business. One such patient was Frederick Lionel Rapson[36] who was admitted to Arrowe Hall in 1916. He had been a driver for the King's Messenger Service in France in 1914. He claimed he had been injured by a blow to the head on 12 March 1915 from a rifle butt in circumstances that were not explained. By early May 1915 he had been invalided to the nearby St. Omer base when noise (or concussion as he termed it) from heavy artillery rendered him unconscious. He was soon returned to England and moved to Woolwich Barracks to recuperate. At his own insistence and on the recommendation of Lord Ilchester of the King's Messenger Service, he was discharged to enable him to join the Mechanical Transport Division of the Union Defence Force in South Africa as a Staff Sergeant. The reason for this particular choice of combat zone is unknown.

Misfortune struck again when he was invalided due to the effects of heat. His Army record states *'fits induced by a blood clot on the brain, probably caused by the blow earlier in the year'*. He returned to England on 17 July 1915 and was transferred to Arrowe Hall. By May 1916, largely recovered and awaiting his army discharge, he was employed by the Red Cross Society Motor Ambulance Department where he was described as *'A most useful man to motor depot'*.[37]

In one account, Miss Schintz claimed to have taken him on to entertain the injured soldiers, but she later claimed to have met him when he replied to her advertisement for a chauffeur. Maybe Dora wanted to replace the chauffeur that had been involved in the accident the previous year. Whatever the circumstances of his employment, his address from September 1916 was *'The Garage'* at Childwall Hall. By 1918 he had a team of men working under him on the Schintz fleet of cars.

Rapson is seen demonstrating his engine powered Rapid jacks on the Schintz 1914 Silver Ghost in the stable yard at Childwall Hall.
The Autocar, 28 July 1917

The Garage at Childwall Hall in 1919. Left to right, probably the 100 h.p. Benz used for tests at Brooklands, and Silver Ghosts LE4107 (probably chassis 1737), LR6392 (21CB) and K294 (5EB). Mechanics in the foreground are checking one of Rapson's inventions, a hood winding system.

The Autocar, 22nd March 1919

It was from this point onwards that the lives of Dora and Frederick Rapson became inextricably linked. Rapson was not only an experienced driver and mechanic but also a prolific inventor, principally of devices for motor cars and he soon started publishing articles to advertise his inventions. He was brimming with ideas and Dora gave him the opportunity, funds, and facilities at Childwall Hall to pursue his interests and carry out experiments. His wartime experiences of driving on the Western Front led Rapson to devise solutions to the problems he had encountered; for example, permanent engine-powered lifting jacks, unpuncturable and/or long-lasting tyres, frictionless screw threads, and miscellaneous coachwork and accessory fittings. In general his designs tended towards safety and convenience.

With financial backing from Dora, his inventions accumulated, and in June 1919 he formed Rapson Automobile Patents Ltd to exploit what was claimed to be 200 Rapson patents. However, this figure could have included overseas registrations or patent applications that subsequently did not find Patent Office acceptance.

HURTWOOD EDGE

Hurtwood Edge c. 1910.
www.alamy.de

By the Autumn of 1919 Dora had purchased a lease on a property called Hurtwood Edge near Cranleigh in Surrey. This had been built in 1910 by Mr A.T. Bolton in an Italianate style and set in woodlands. In July 1923 Dora had it valued at £6,500 with a view to using it as security against a loan. In the event, she appears to have sold the lease later that year. Why Dora purchased this property is not known and it is doubtful if she ever lived there. Much later this property became the home of the guitarist, Eric Clapton.

OTTERSHAW PARK

Shortly after acquiring Hurtwood Edge Dora leased Ottershaw Park near Chertsey, Surrey from its owner, Friedrich Gustav Jonathan Eckstein, and took up residence there with her mother in May 1920. The Ottershaw estate was considerably the more imposing of the two properties, with a mansion, built between 1910 and 1913, of some 91 rooms and a frontage of 375 feet. It was designed by Niven & Wigglesworth in Palladian style, steel-framed and faced with Bath stone and replaced an earlier mansion dating back to the 1760s which Eckstein had had demolished. It was a very imposing structure dubbed '*The Wonder House of Surrey*'[38] by the press and was said to have one of the most magnificent interiors in England.[39]

Ottershaw Park Mansion shortly after its construction in c.1913.
From a postcard

Collection of Miss Schintz's Hackney trophies on display in the Mansion at Ottershaw.
Annabel Collenette

Dora's dining room at Ottershaw Park with her hackney driving trophies displayed on the far table.
From 1931 sale particulars

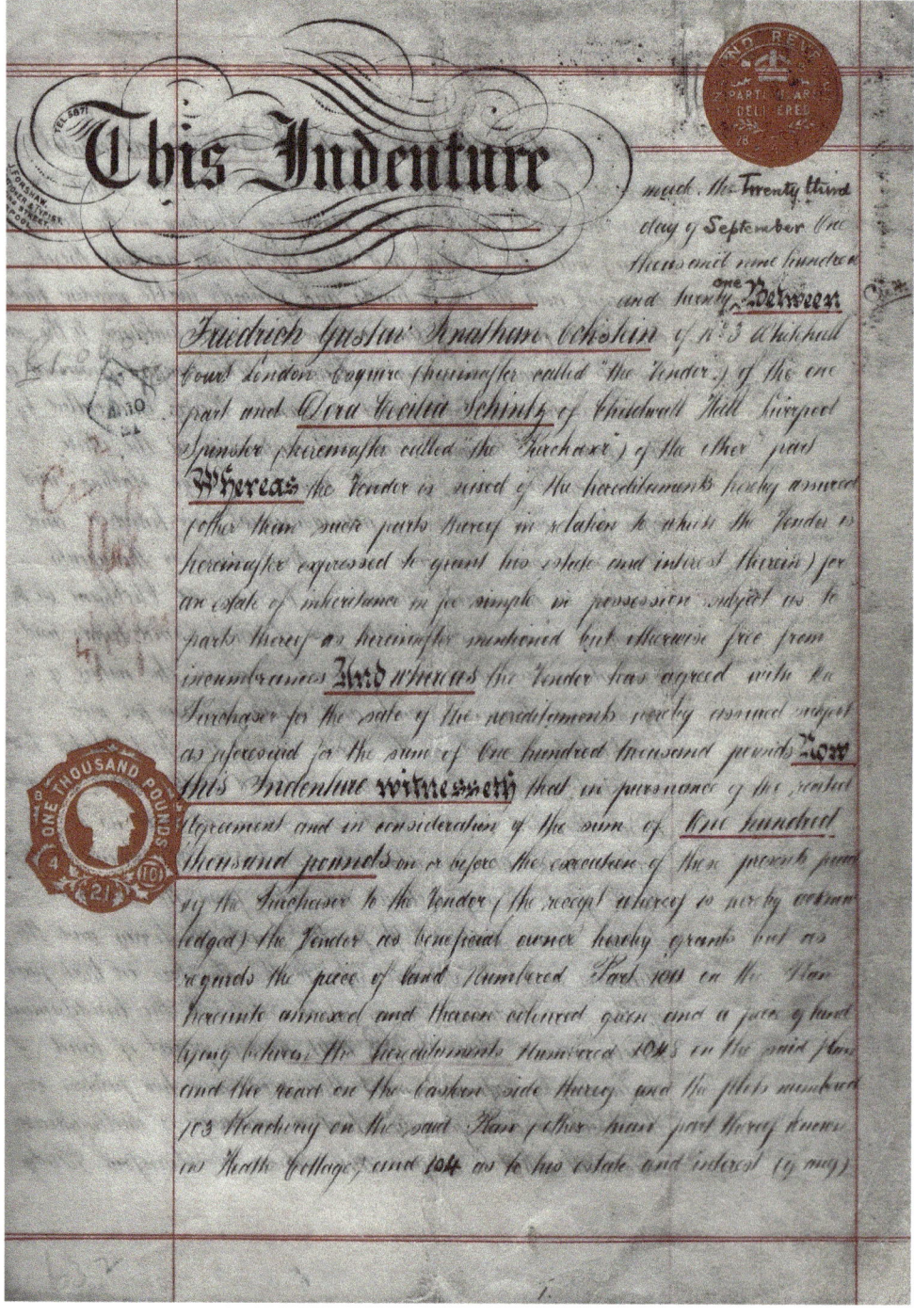

First page of document relating to conveyance of Ottershaw Park from Friedrich Eckstein to Dora Schintz dated 23rd September 1921.

The estate extended to about 1000 acres including formal gardens, pleasure grounds, a number of ponds, a deer park, estate workers' cottages and several outlying farms.

According to the June 1921 census Dora had a dozen indoor servants including a housekeeper, a cook, a dressmaker, five house maids, a kitchen maid, a scullery maid, a hall boy and an odd man[40] many of whom had come with her from Childwall Hall. Also listed in the census return as visitors were Ada Whitehouse, who was described as an *invalid*, and Grace Morgan, a nurse, who had worked at Arrowe Hall and was presumably there to look after her.

Frederick Rapson was also listed as a resident in the mansion at this time. He was accompanied south from Childwall Hall by four other chauffeurs, Frederick Boorer and William Burkey together with William Cash and Charles Chapman with their wives. Dora's gardeners from Thickthorn, Alfred Dyer and his uncle, Arthur Lawrence, together with their families also joined her at Ottershaw. These employees lived over the garages in The Bothy or in other properties on the estate.

However, it was not until 23 September 1921, and after some legal wrangling with Eckstein in the High Court about the condition of the electricity and water supplies, that the entire estate was finally conveyed to her. The Ottershaw estate cost Dora £100,000 (equivalent to about £3 million today) and she spent an additional £25,000 on improvements. She later claimed to have moved to Ottershaw for the sake of her elderly mother who had suffered emotionally from the tragic deaths of her son and husband, and because she believed her mother would benefit from the beautiful Surrey countryside. However, it is possible that this move south was engineered by Rapson so as to be only a few miles from the Brooklands racetrack which he later used for testing his emerging tyre designs. He was also close to the Richmond premises of David Oyler who was commissioned to make tyres for Rapson before he acquired his own factory in New Malden in 1921, funded at great expense by Dora.

Having moved south, in 1921 Rapson moved into a house at 2 Acacia Road in fashionable St. John's Wood, London. This must have been paid for by Dora. Here his wife, Rose, and his children lived with a nanny and two other servants. Rapson ran his infant business from the workshops in The Bothy on the Ottershaw estate. He had an apartment in the mansion and used the Acacia Road address for his days in London. His eldest son, Freddie, attended nearby Arnold House School and later University College, London, his education no doubt also being funded by Dora.

Dora still owned hackneys after the move to Ottershaw and she displayed her many championship cups in her dining room. Now retired from the show ring she drove her horses locally for her own enjoyment and local residents recalled seeing her driving high-stepping horses around the estate. Some of these animals may have been her favourite show horses from Thickthorn and were most likely stabled locally at Dolly's Farm.

It was said that she would often walk around the estate and across the fields. She called one young lad, the son of an estate worker, '*her blue eyes*' and at Christmas she arranged for him and all the other estate workers' children to be driven in one of her Rolls-Royces to tea and the pantomime.

In 1924 Dora conveyed a plot of land at the back of Ottershaw Church specifically for the burial of her staff.[41] Only three burials took place here. Russell Gooch Fry, one of her motor mechanics, was interred in 1926 and Kate and Robert Pickett the wife and son of John Pickett an estate carter were buried in 1925 and 1927, respectively. Part of this plot was reserved for Dora and her heirs but was never used for this purpose.

On 22 September 1921, the day before the Ottershaw estate was finally conveyed to Dora, her mother died. She was cremated at Woking Crematorium[42] and according to their records her ashes were sent to Anfield Crematorium in Liverpool although no record of them arriving has so far been found.

A CASE OF TRESPASS

The previous owner of Ottershaw Park Estate, Friedrich Eckstein, had employed a Mr. Charles Winslow Taylor, a butler turned house agent, as an estate manager and had four estate cottages at Dunford (or Durnford) converted into accommodation for him in 1910.

In February 1912, friction developed between Taylor and a Miss Mary Read, who had been engaged as a housekeeper, over the management of the estate. Taylor finally brought an action for slander against her in the High Court in 1913 which, unfortunately for him, failed. Although Eckstein found him honourable and hardworking and had no complaint against him, he was nevertheless dismissed in December that year. After this, his house, then called Durnford Lodge, was occupied by a succession of estate managers until November 1926 when Dora sold the property - to the same Charles Taylor.

It appears that Dora and Taylor were on friendly terms, as in 1927 she confided in him about the '*unfortunate relationship both personal and financial with Frederick Rapson*' and frequently consulted him about estate matters and her personal financial affairs. This was despite the fact that Rapson had by now assumed the role of Dora's business advisor. One can detect in this the likelihood that Dora did not wish to rely entirely on Rapson's advice. Taylor was on such good terms with her that he even loaned her £6000 on one occasion to free her from a debt to money lenders.

In August 1927 Dora was prosecuted by Surrey County Council for not complying with a notice to carry out work to remove silt from the Bourne and Little Bourne, the streams separating the estate from Taylor's land and was fined £57.15s.0d at Chertsey Police Court. Taylor offered to carry out the necessary work and Dora was pleased to accept on the understanding that it would not cost her anything. The relationship between the two continued to be very amicable until early in 1928 when, by reason of various undisclosed petty differences, relations became strained. Taylor was continuing the work on the water courses, for which he believed he had permission, when Dora entered his garden shouting and accusing him of trespass and being a disgrace to the county and the village. She called him a nuisance and said that everybody asked her why she had sold Durnford Lodge to such an awful man.

This outburst was followed two days later by the erection of no fewer than twenty-two signs on her property facing towards Taylor's land each bearing the inscription *Strictly Private*. Taylor was so annoyed by this change of attitude after all he had done for her, without charge, that he retaliated by adding the words *Asylum Grounds* to two of the signs as in his view what Dora had done was '*not the act of a person whose mind was evenly balanced*'. Dora's head gardener, Harry King, removed the signs, but Taylor erected another sign, much bigger than the previous ones but with the same wording and in full view of passers-by on the Guildford Road and from Durnford Bridge. According to witnesses this gave the impression that the estate grounds were those of a *Lunatic Asylum*.

Dora brought an injunction against Taylor in the High Court in August 1928[43], alleging that he had cut back the banks of the stream separating his property from the estate and had trespassed on her land in order to do so. Before the case could be heard she issued further threats that trespassers would be thrown into the Bourne and that two men had been put on guard for this purpose. As a final act of annoyance she had a caravan parked close by his drawing room windows. The court ordered the signs to be removed but it is not known how this debacle was concluded.

THE CARS

Late in life Dora commented that her only hobby was motoring. It is likely that she didn't drive herself but relied on the services of chauffeurs. She certainly only ever owned high-quality makes of car. Many of these were purchased so that Rapson could experiment with various fixtures and fittings he had invented.

The c.1912 Sheffield Simplex which by 1915 had been re-bodied and loaned to the Red Cross for ambulance work probably came from her late father's fleet. It is likely she had a Rolls-Royce Silver Ghost with Rothschild coachwork registered LE-4107 even before meeting Rapson. If she did not buy it herself then this too might have been one of her father's cars. It was not sold until 1928, suggesting it was her favourite and by the 1920s it had been modernised or rebodied as a full cabriolet.

Over the ensuing years, her fleet of cars grew to include several of the grandest British makes, including other Rolls-Royces and examples of Lanchester, Napier, Daimler and Austin, most maintained and chauffeured by Rapson's team.

While at Childwall Hall, Dora had acquired a 1914 Rolls-Royce Silver Ghost registered K-294. This carried Watson of Liverpool torpedo coachwork. By 1917 it had been rebodied[44], no doubt at Rapson's behest, as a Mulliner centre-door saloon. The Watson torpedo body was not wasted and seems to have been fitted to Dora's next car, a 1915 Silver Ghost registered K-239 acquired in late 1918. Both cars were sold during 1921-22.

Dora's 1915 Silver Ghost K-239 chassis no. 32RD outside the Guildhall School of Music, John Carpenter Street in London.

John Fasal

Also at Childwall Hall, Dora indulged Rapson by paying for an old 100 h.p. Benz, which was more of a plaything than a means of transport. It and several Rolls-Royces accompanied the move south to Ottershaw.

The third Rolls-Royce bought by Dora was a 1915 Silver Ghost registered LR-6392, a Barker tourer. This chassis had been intended for the Czar of Russia but war meant it became available to the home market. Like many of her cars, it was registered in Rapson's name but Dora was undoubtedly the real purchaser. This car was soon rebodied as a coupe.

In 1919, Dora added another 1914 Silver Ghost, a limousine, to her fleet but it was sold as early as 1921. Around 1920 a 1912 Silver Ghost, bodied by a London coachbuilder as a torpedo or coupe, was acquired.

In 1920 Dora purchased her first new post-war Silver Ghost, believed to be the tourer registered in Surrey as PC-5877, bodied as a Barker torpedo and sold before 1926.

Dora's fleet of cars with chauffeurs in The Bothy at Ottershaw Park, c.1921. Left to right, 1915 Silver Ghost bulbous coupe LR-6392 (21CB), Daimler XA-2722, Ghost LE-4107, a Lanchester cabriolet, 1921 Napier PB-8232, 1921 Ghost PB-7863 bulbous coupe (70JG) and 1920 Ghost PC-5877 (70YE). Most of the cars carry Rapson's eagle mascot.

Car and Golf 10 March 1922

The most memorable of Dora's cars was her 1921 Silver Ghost, briefly registered LE-4107 (taken from the c.1912 car described earlier) but finally registered PB-7863. It was a Barker coupe in a special bulbous Rapson style.

Despite growing money worries, in 1926 Rapson prevailed on Dora to buy one of the latest Rolls-Royces, a Phantom I, a Windovers coupe, registered as YP-4286. A huge indulgence was another Lanchester paid for by Dora, a 1922 40 h.p. racer used by Rapson to test his unpuncturable tyres.

Whilst her money paid for most of the cars only some were for day-to-day use. Dora was probably chauffeured in the Napier or possibly the Daimler as both had enclosed bodies, but if she could drive herself then one small car was available, a 1926 Austin 7, which she may have preferred.

FINANCIAL PROBLEMS

Rapson's business activities were burgeoning in the early 1920s and he needed a continual flow of investment to underwrite his new enterprises. Over the years between £250,000 and £350,000 (current equivalent to £20-30 million) of Dora's wealth went into Rapson's companies. To raise money to sponsor Rapson and to pay off various debts, she mortgaged her properties at Thickthorn and Ottershaw for at least £173,000, but her gross income was only £22,854. After tax and interest to be paid on the mortgages, she was left virtually penniless.

Indeed, Dora's financial troubles seem to have started soon after she arrived at Ottershaw as, in November 1921, it was reported that the outlying portions of the estate, some 464 acres, were to be sold at auction. As it turned out, some of the land, including Bonsey's Farm, was sold privately in advance of the sale on 10 August 1922, but the remaining 326 acres failed to find a buyer.

To raise money in 1922 Dora was advised to sell some of the Auby shares she had inherited from her father. She received £53,000 for them but later she discovered that they had been undervalued and should have fetched about four times that amount.

> SALE THURSDAY NEXT (10th August),
> at the ALBION HOTEL, WOKING,
> at 11 a.m.
>
> BY DIRECTION OF MISS DORA C. SCHINTZ.
>
> ## SURREY.
>
> About 2½ and 3 miles respectively from Chertsey and Woking Junction Stations. London can be reached in about 35 minutes by a frequent service of trains.
>
> OUTLYING PORTIONS OF THE
>
> ## OTTERSHAW PARK ESTATE,
>
> comprising
>
> DOLLEY'S HOUSE,
> A Country Residence.
> Also
> THREE CAPITAL AGRICULTURAL HOLDINGS,
> possessing considerable prospective value, being equipped with suitable Dwelling Houses and Buildings,
> known as
>
> Lot 1.—SCOTCHERS FARM .. .. 80½ Acres.
> ,, 3.—DOLLEY'S FARM .. .. 126½ ,,
> ,, 7.—DUNFORD FARM .. .. 78 ,,
> Also Accommodation Lands and Cottages, the whole extending to an area of over
>
> 326 ACRES.
>
> Solicitors :—Messrs. GODFREY WARR and Co., 85, Gracechurch-street, E.C.3.
>
> Auctioneers :—Messrs. KNIGHT, FRANK and RUTLEY, 20, Hanover-square, W.1.

Notice of sale of outlying portions of Ottershaw Park Estate.
The Times 3 August 1922

In a further attempt to obtain funds Dora mortgaged the Ottershaw estate in August 1923 for £77,000. This was followed in March 1924 by a charge of £16,000 and in December that year and by a further charge of £18,000. These appear to have been loans arranged by the Warr, Cole and Hay an established firm of London solicitors.

By 1926 Thickthorn had still not sold. Dora had previously mortgaged the property, but she needed more money to support Rapson's business ventures.

Financial advice was by now provided by Joseph Wyatt, managing clerk at Messrs Hore, Pattison & Bathurst, solicitors. Wyatt was first introduced to Rapson in March 1925 by Arthur Keston who was a director of the Rapson Tyre and Jack Company, and who together with Rapson was advising Dora with respect both to her interests in the company and her private affairs. The object of the introduction was to ascertain whether Wyatt could procure finance for Rapson's company and Wyatt must have seen a way of doing this through loans on the security of Dora's properties.

Wyatt was in partnership with a retired naval captain, James Pask, but neither was a registered money lender. Between 1926 and 1929 Dora took out twelve more mortgages arranged by Wyatt and Pask[45]. She borrowed from other lenders as well but several of these loans were transferred to Wyatt. Most of this money found its way to Rapson or one of his companies. Rapson also borrowed money and Dora often had to pay off his bank overdrafts and debts when lenders began proceedings to recover the loans.

When she eventually realised that she had been defrauded, in 1931 Dora began a court case[46] in an attempt to protect her assets. Records of the court proceedings are extremely complex and reveal a detailed account of her financial situation over the preceding years. In her submission to the Court of Chancery Dora alleged that Wyatt and Pask (who was deceased by the time of the trial) together with Rapson contrived to influence her into executing the mortgages with the intention of acquiring her properties. She also claimed that she had been induced to lend very large sums to, and make significant investments in, Rapson and his companies.

Dora alleged that Wyatt had complained to her that she did not carry out the advice he gave and suggested that she appoint an attorney. Naturally she chose Rapson but later she claimed that he had arranged some loans against her will. She further alleged that Wyatt received considerable commission payments from insurance companies and from Rapson, and that he led an extravagant lifestyle at her expense incurring debts at restaurants and in hiring Daimler limousines.

These accusations seem at odds with Dora's later assertion that Rapson was innocent of any wrongdoing. Later, when interviewed, at no time did she blame him for her financial ruin although the press played heavily on this suggestion. Maybe these claims were just intended to strengthen her court case.

To complicate matters further, a Mary Jane Colville-Hyde was added as a defendant to the action when she found out that money lent by Wyatt and Pask was substantially from a trust fund of which she was a beneficiary and they were trustees.

Dora asked the court to declare the money lending illegal, to cancel the mortgages and to issue injunctions restraining Wyatt from foreclosing on the loans or from benefitting from sales of the mortgaged properties.

Share certificate of the Auby Company.

In his defence Wyatt denied all the allegations and claimed that Dora was at all times aware of the liabilities she was undertaking and that he had never used any undue influence over her.

In the end the matter was settled out of court and so the truth will never be known. The press had a field day over the court proceedings and news of the case was syndicated worldwide reaching papers as far afield as Estonia and Australia.

Dora was a shareholder and trustee of the Auby Company. In 1927, in another legal battle over her finances, she was the plaintiff in a complex lawsuit against the other trustees of the company who included her own sister and brother-in-law. This related to a decision in 1924 by the company, which was effectively owned by the Schintz family, to recapitalise the company using reserves. She claimed that as a trustee she had never been consulted by the others about this proposed arrangement. Furthermore, she had not agreed to it since it would not be in her interests to do so as she relied on the income from dividends paid out of capital. She claimed that the other trustees had acted fraudulently and in breach of trust. However, after a three-day hearing in the High Court, it was decided that the case was outside the jurisdiction of the court and that the matter should be decided by the Douai Commercial Court in France. The case appears to have been dismissed with costs payable by Dora.

In an attempt to pay off the mortgages and other debts, Dora then attempted to release the capital of her settlement and inheritance trusts. However, this was opposed in a court case in 1928 by her sister's family. They objected because, under the terms of the trusts, the capital would pass ultimately to her sister and her children. In view of her past history, there must have been some concern that Dora would spend all the money before it could be passed on.

There is a record of two van loads of paintings being taken to Switzerland in 1927 for Dora and payment being made to a third party in respect of a trip there to advise on their value.[46] It appears that fearing her impending bankruptcy Dora was setting aside some tangible investments for a rainy day.

BANKRUPTCY

Dora eventually filed for bankruptcy in July 1930 with liabilities of £238,000, and Ottershaw Park was put in the hands of trustees to be sold off at auction. The contents were auctioned in October 1930 and the estate sold over the next two years through a number of private sales to speculators.

The estate auction catalogue provides detailed descriptions of the rooms at this time and shows the extravagant surroundings that Dora had been living in. The Dining Room is described as:

> 'An unusually handsome room about 45ft by 23ft also enjoying, in common with the other reception rooms, wide and beautiful views of the Italian Garden, the Park, and the Hills beyond. The dining Room is completely panelled in oak, ornamented by carvings in the style of Grinling Gibbons. The ceilings are supported by fluted Ionic pillars with fine carved capitals. A central panel of the ceiling is painted with cloud and sky effects, surrounded by gilded carvings in high relief after Grinling Gibbons. The cornice is ornamented by modillions and enriched with acanthus, egg-and-dart, and oak leaf designs. The open fireplace has a black marble hearth with grey marble chimneypiece. The floor is of oak parquetry.'[47]

The sale of effects took place over five days and the auction catalogue provides interesting detail of the contents room-by-room. For example, the list of furniture and soft furnishings in the Dining Room included a pink Wilton super pile carpet, 35ft x 19ft, a dark oak dining table, 4ft square, an oak table 2ft square, an oak table 3ft 6in square, a pink ground pile figured and bordered rugs, 7ft x 4ft and 6ft x 3ft, a Louis XV kingwood commode with ormolu enrichments, fitted with a marble top, one drawer and cupboard under.[48]

The catalogue also lists four vehicles: an old Benz motor car (£4, sold for aluminium scrap to a Mr. Pucci), a 1926 Austin 7 (£19.10.0), the 1922 Lanchester saloon PD-6682 (£82), and a Napier farm lorry MD-9090 (£10.10.0). Dora was permitted to use the Rolls-Royce cabriolet (LE-4107) and the valuable Phantom I coupe (YP-4286), although they were still held as security against other money owed to her solicitors.

In the same month the entire estate was offered at auction but only outlying farms were sold. At a subsequent auction in May 1931 several small plots including one of the farm cottages in Bonsey's Lane, land on the western side of the estate, the North Lodges and a plot on Chobham Road were sold but there were no bidders for the rest of the estate. These were sold in 1932 to the Ottershaw Park Investment Company. They leased and then sold the mansion and central part of the park to Ottershaw College, a newly established boarding school for boys, in 1934.

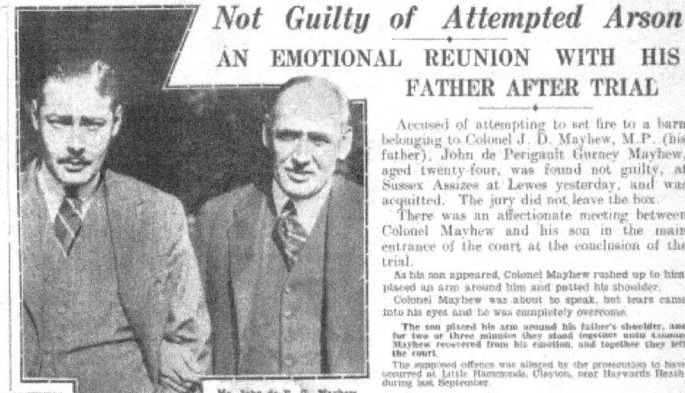

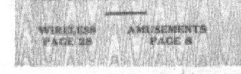

Front page news – The Daily Mirror on 10 December 1932 featured the story of Dora's bankruptcy.

Times must have been hard throughout these years for Dora. However, her benevolence and funds were not entirely exhausted as she hosted a number of fêtes and shows in the estate grounds in aid of various charities including the Ottershaw Nurses Fund and the Working Men's Club right up until 1927. Another example of her generosity was recalled by a resident of Ottershaw who remembered that in the 1920s her mother had a brain tumour removed and that Dora paid the cost of the operation.

Before she left Ottershaw a visit by a newspaper correspondent in August 1930 found that she was very ill and not receiving visitors, her manservant saying that her doctor had been urgently summoned.[49]

On leaving Ottershaw in 1930 she had sixteen of her horses shot to prevent them falling into the hands of someone who might mistreat them.[25]

> **TO-MORROW (SATURDAY) IS THE GREAT DAY FOR OTTERSHAW & DISTRICT.**
>
> SPLENDID ENTRIES have been received (including 160 in the four classes for Dogs, and 100 entries in other live stock; many in the mice, Cats and Guinea Pig sections.
>
> **Come and Enjoy Yourself.**
>
> OTTERSHAW and DISTRICT
> **FETE and SHOW**
> In Aid of the Ottershaw Nurse Fund will be held in
> **OTTERSHAW PARK**
> (By kind permission of Miss D. Schintz)
> **TO-MORROW, SATURDAY, JULY 16th.**
>
> THE GORDON BOYS' AND ADDLESTONE BANDS.
> Flowers, Fruit and Vegetables.
> Dogs (by permission of the Kennel Club), Poultry, Rabbits, Cats, Rats, Cavies, Mice and Goats.
> BEAUTY and BABY COMPETITIONS.
> Fancy Dress (Adults' and Children's ditto).
> CHILDREN'S SPORTS.
> Good Prizes and many Specials for all Sections.
> DANCING.   GRAND CONCERT.
> Cocoanut Shies and Side Shows of all descriptions
>
> Shilling tickets may be obtained before the day at 9d. each (children half-price); also schedules from the following: Addlestone, Messrs. T. Snelgrove, Estate Agent, Turner's Stores, T. Durrant, Burleigh Park; Chertsey, Miss Taylor, fruiterer, London Street, Messrs. Ridler, butcher, Guildford Street; Chobham, Messrs. Benham and Sons, The Stores; Woking, Messrs. Wearing, M.P.S., Chobham Road; Miss Statter, Westfield; Weybridge, Messrs. Haslett, drapers, Church Street; Ottershaw, Messrs. Thompson, The Dairy, Mr. Latham, The Otter, Mr. Goldring, the Post Office, Mr. W. S. Hunt, Coal Merchant, Mr. Stride, ironmonger.
> Manager: W. S. HUNT, Ottershaw.
> Hon. Sec.: A. T. SLEET, Ottershaw.

Advertisement to fête and show in Ottershaw Park.
Surrey Herald 15 July 1927

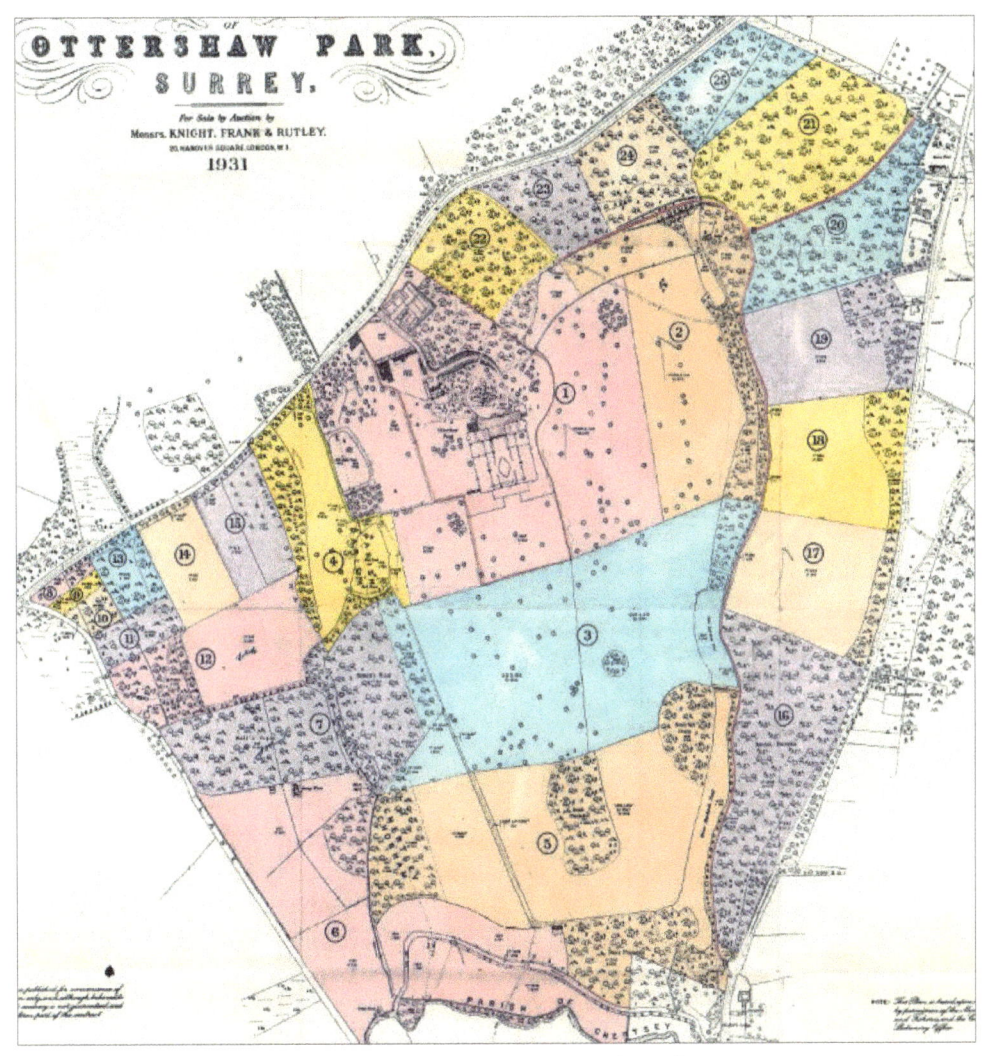

The Ottershaw Park estate as portrayed in the 1931 auction catalogue with the various plots available for sale.

SURREY

CLOSE TO SUNNINGDALE, CHERTSEY AND WOKING.

About two miles from Chertsey and three miles from Woking.

Particulars, Plan, Views and Conditions of Sale

OF THE

Freehold Palatial and Famous County Seat

KNOWN AS

Ottershaw Park

extending to about

432 Acres.

To be offered for SALE by AUCTION as a WHOLE or in BLOCKS or LOTS by Messrs.

KNIGHT, FRANK & RUTLEY

(Sir Howard Frank, Bart., G.B.E., K.C.B., F.S.I.; Alfred J. Burrows, F.S.I., P.P.A.I.; Arthur Horace Knight, F.A.I.; and William Gibson, D.S.O., F.S.I.),

---

At the Estate Room, No. 20, Hanover Square, London, W.1,

On THURSDAY, the 21st day of MAY, 1931

At 2.30 o'clock
(unless previously disposed of privately).

SOLICITORS : Messrs. KENNETH BROWN, BAKER, BAKER,
Essex House, Essex Street, Strand, London, W.C.2.
'Phone : Temple Bar 2871.

INCORPORATED ACCOUNTANTS : Messrs. KEENS, SHAY, KEENS & CO.,
Bilbao House, New Broad Street, London, E.C.2 ;
and at Luton and Bedford.
'Phone : London Wall 9320.

AUCTIONEERS : Messrs. KNIGHT, FRANK & RUTLEY,
20, Hanover Square, London, W.1 ;
and at Edinburgh and Ashford, Kent.
Phone : Mayfair 3771.

Front page of 1931 auction catalogue for sale of Ottershaw Park.

EASTBOURNE

Frederick Rapson, his family and nanny moved to Eastbourne where his wife Rose's spinster sister lived and Dora soon followed, presumably to be near the Rapsons who she later described as the only true friends she ever had.

The trauma of the bankruptcy resulted in Dora spending the next two years virtually bedridden at the St John's Private Hotel in Eastbourne, suffering from what would appear to be depression. She was due to appear in court for a public examination on October 1930[50] but due to her ill-health this was postponed until May 1931 and thereafter indefinitely. An article in the Daily Mail on 10 December 1932 reported:

> *'Miss Schintz has for two years been bedridden at a quiet Eastbourne hotel weak and ill and is constantly attended by a doctor. She is known as the mystery woman owing to her reticence and refusal to mix with other guests. A resident at the hotel told me Miss Schintz has been seen only on one or two occasions since I have been here. On each occasion she was coming out of her room and immediately ran back as if frightened.'*[51]

Another report from the same paper two days later painted a picture of a very sick woman:

> 'A shaded light at the side of her huge old-fashioned bed threw a soft glow over her sunken features. One thin hand lay outside the coverlet. Her voice held a note of weariness and sometimes sank to a whisper.'[52]

As if money troubles were not enough, while at the hotel she was attended by the notorious Dr. John Bodkin Adams, who is believed to have killed 160 of his patients. He benefited from their wills and faced a murder charge in 1957 but was acquitted. There is, however, no evidence that Adams was in any way responsible for Dora's prolonged illness. Whether she was in his sights as a potential victim remains speculation. Maybe he became aware of her dire financial situation.

Rapson's name featured prominently in all the national newspapers as the Schintz litigation continued and it must have been devastating for him to see his reputation impugned.

In 1933 Dora moved from the hotel to Aymond Grange at 8 Dittons Road, Eastbourne. Rapson was staying at this address with his wife and son for a few days to help with the move but on 6 September he died aged just 43 years. His death certificate shows that epilepsy and the fracture to the back of his skull received in 1915 were the cause of his demise.

At the time of Rapson's death Dora told the press *'He used to call me 'angel'. His friendship was the only happiness I have ever known. He was so clever and brilliant and I was happy for him to manage my affairs and to back his tyre business. Now he lies in a shroud that I made myself.'*[53]

A reporter who visited her at Aymond Grange, found her keeping vigil over his coffin wrote:

> 'I found Miss Schintz's house with drawn blinds and tightly closed windows. She opened the door to me – an ill, trembling figure, thin to emaciation, nerves torn out of her. […] It was hard to believe that this shabby, pathetic figure wandering like a shadow around the quiet house was once the owner of a magnificent mansion in Surrey […]'

At that time she said '*He soon became invaluable to me. He managed all my affairs [...]. He was my memory, my eyesight, everything to me. His friendship and help gave me the only real happiness I have known. I was always alone. I preferred it like that. People gave me no happiness nor did things. My only hobby was breeding horses*'.[54]

The picture of her in the Daily Mail 10 December 1932 when the Rapson affair made the headlines was evidently taken many years earlier at Arrowe Hall as she is wearing the same clothes as seen in the wartime group photo. By the standards of the day this photograph of her reclining on the ground was fairly provocative and presumably meant to imply that her involvement with Rapson was not just of a financial kind. There is no evidence that there was any romantic entanglement between them, but the press made mileage out of their close relationship and implied there was a liaison between the two with newspaper headlines such as '*War-time Romance*'. However, she was quoted as saying that '*He was my friend, always with the consent of his wife*'[55] which suggests the relationship was platonic.

A special picture of Miss Susan Dora Cecelia Schintz.

Photograph of Dora Schintz thought to have been taken during WW1 at Arrowe Hall when she would have been aged about 46 years.
Daily Mail 10 December 1932

His cremation took place in Woking Crematorium on 11 September 1933[56]. It is said that Dora and not his widow, Rose, carried the casket containing his ashes back home to Eastbourne but his final resting place is not known.

**Bolsover Court, Eastbourne in 2008, where
Dora staged her legal comeback.**

1935-38 was the period of Dora's final legal battle. During this time, she lived in the attic apartment no.7 at Bolsover Court in Bolsover Road, Eastbourne, accompanied only by Ellen Wilson, who had been her maid at Ottershaw. From here she staged a legal comeback in order to obtain a discharge from bankruptcy and to clear her name and Rapson's. Freddie, Rapson's eldest son, now acted as Dora's driver and secretary in place of his father and spent months with Dora typing a fifty-page dossier setting out in detail her finances in preparation for her court appearance. In a front page newspaper article she said in November 1936:

> 'I shall fight myself to clear the name of a brilliant honest man who was shockingly ill-treated, and so that his son shall not have to bear the stigma of a father who was called a swindler. I am not doing it for myself. There is no happiness for me now after what I have gone through. Even when I was wealthy I was never really content... money does not buy happiness.'[57]

In January 1937 Dora, now frail and grey-haired, finally faced a public examination at Kingston-upon-Thames County Court during which details of her financial affairs were reviewed. During the proceedings it became clear that she had very little understanding of financial matters. The court took a lenient attitude and she was discharged from bankruptcy in August 1938, thus ending some 20 tumultuous years as the backer of a minor industrialist.

One of the last known photographs of Dora Schintz aged 68.
Daily Express 13 January 1937

SWITZERLAND

With the Second World War approaching, Dora moved to a Villa in Leuggern, Switzerland from where she wrote to her cousin Beatrice Burkly and her daughter, Betty. Early in the war she wrote that Hitler was not so bad as the English thought, saying that having read the German newspapers and listened to the German radio, she thought that he was '*neither a madman nor wicked*' – but this may have been inserted to ensure that the letter got through German censorship. By now Dora was financially dependent on a monthly allowance from her brother-in-law, John Moreton, which was barely enough to support her as she wrote in 1943:

> *'I have my usual monthly remittance regularly from my brother-in-law. Just under half what I used to have. My rent has also been reduced till the war is over so I suppose I will be turned out then. I just manage to squeeze through every month but it is no use worrying. So long as I don't get into debt. All the trades people are really nice and sympathetic. If I am "broke" before the end of the month I borrow from my grocer who understands my position.'*[58]

After the war, Dora returned to England where she stayed at the luxurious Piccadilly Hotel, London. She very likely attended Betty Burkly's wedding to John Freeman in West Ealing on 20 April 1946. While here she also wrote her final will on 31 April but by September she had returned to Switzerland, flying from Croydon to Lucerne. She later wrote to Betty to say that she had found a chalet to lease near Hertenstein on the shores of Lake Lucerne. A transcription of this letter is as follows:

Chalet Oresseli Hertenstein, Luzern Sep 22nd 46

Dear Betty

At last I have found a small place to rest. I have taken the above chalet and am moving my furniture in next Tuesday. It is not one of the artistic chalets one sees about in fact it is on the ugly side but very clean inside and fairly modern. Good bathroom etc. It is half the size of my last villa near Luzern but one has to think of the cost and the rent. It is quite near the lake only a narrow road in between. Perhaps you have been to this hotel Hertenstein and know the road. It is about 2 miles from Weggis where you stayed I believe. There are many villas about here but all owned by people who have money and do not need to let. They shut them up for the winter. Besides they are all furnished and I would have had to pay or storage as well as rent.

Reverse of envelope showing Nazi and British censors had read Dora's letter to Beatrice Burkly.

I had a very good flight from Croydon on Sep 2nd, stayed in Luzern for a week and then came here. It is a nice hotel and restaurant owned by an Austrian, but of course like all Swiss country hotels, noisy. The uncarpeted floors are terrible and people tramp about above you and one can't sleep so I am looking forward to my own bed and complete solitude with great eagerness as you can imagine. I hope your visit to the docks was satisfactory and that the content of the trunk was good. I thoroughly enjoyed the tea we had thanks to your energetic efforts. My adventures in England seem like a dream. Certainly it turned out a quite useless expense and aged me quite 10 years both in appearance and spirit. I hope your mother and you will get through the winter alright. There is [...] no coal or coke for private use here.

Yours
Dora Schinz[59]

THE FINAL YEARS

Dora did not remain long in Switzerland and by 1952 she was back in England. The last two years of her life were spent at Broome Park, a residential hotel between Maidstone and Dover, once the country home of Lord Kitchener, where she had rooms alongside several other elderly residents.

Broome Hall in the earlier 1900s.
Public domain

She died in the Kent and Canterbury Hospital on 12 June 1954 from bronchopneumonia aged 84. As she appeared to have no friends or relatives to take care of her affairs, her sister and brother-in-law having pre-deceased her, Mr A. J. Smithers, a solicitor in the firm of Girling, Wilson & Bailey made funeral arrangements with C.W. Lyons of Canterbury for her cremation (no. 22490) at Charing near Ashford on 23 June 1954. Her remains were scattered on the East Lawn at the crematorium near the 2nd oak opposite the 4th rose bed but there is no permanent memorial to her and no entry in the book of remembrance.

When and where died	Name and surname	Sex	Age	Occupation	Cause of death	Signature, description and residence of informant	When registered
Twelfth June 1954 Kent and Canterbury Hospital U.D.	Susan Dora Cecilia SCHINTZ	Female	84 Years	Broome Park Hotel Barham Bridge Blean R.D. Spinster Of no occupation Daughter of ----- Schintz a ----- (deceased)	Acute Bronchopneumonia Pericarditis Hypertension Certified by C A Gardner Coroner for City and County of Canterbury after Post Mortem without Inquest	A. J. Smithers Causing the body to be buried 32 St Margarets Street Canterbury	Twenty ninth June 1954

Extract from death certificate of Dora Schintz with transcription.

In her will Dora left what little remained (£1774) of her once vast fortune to a number of former employees. Ellen Wilson, her maid, and George Rose, her bailiff from the Thickthorn estate, each received a quarter. The rest was divided between Mrs Rolands, a cook, who had probably been at Childwall Hall; Mrs Dawes, a cook at Ottershaw and wife of James, a carpenter; Mrs Boorer (known as Sister Morgan) who had been matron at Arrowe Hall and who had married Frederick Boorer, one of the Ottershaw chauffeurs in 1926; and Mrs Lawrence, wife of the head gardener at Childwall and Ottershaw. She obviously got on well with her loyal staff and in a letter referred to Mrs Lawrence as a '*nice little woman*'.[60]

And so ended the life of an extraordinary woman....

This is the last Will of me SUSAN DORA CECILIA SCHINTZ at present residing at the Piccadilly Hotel in the County of London Spinster.

1. I APPOINT CHARLES DOUGLAS MEDLEY of 52 Bedford Square in the County of London or failing him JOHN CHRISTOPHER MEDLEY of the same place Solicitor and GEORGE ROSE of 73 Roderick Avenue Peacehaven in the County of Sussex Bailiff to be EXECUTORS AND TRUSTEES of this my Will to each of whom on proof of the Will I BEQUEATH Fifty pounds free of duty.

2. I GIVE AND BEQUEATH all my property of every kind to my Trustees Upon trust to sell and convert the same into money and to hold the moneys arising from the sale and conversion and any moneys of which I may die possessed Upon trust to divide the same into equal moieties and to hold one moiety Upon trust to pay one half to the said George Rose and the other half to Ellen Wilson (ladies maid) of 20 Sandhurst Road Aigburth Road Liverpool/and to stand possessed of the other moiety Upon trust to divide the same in equal shares between the following or the survivors or survivor thereof namely :-

Mrs. Rolands (Cook) of 16 Sherwood Road Wallasey Cheshire
Mrs. Dawes (Cook) of The Laurels, Ottershaw Woking Surrey
Mrs. Boorea (Sister Morgan) of Glen Garth Lingfield Surrey and
Mrs. Lawrence (Gardener's Wife) Garden Court Cottage Ottershaw aforesaid

IN WITNESS whereof I have hereunto set my hand this 30th day of August - one thousand nine hundred and forty six.

SIGNED by the said Susan Dora Cecilia Schintz the Testatrix as and for her Last Will in the presence of us both being present at the same time who at her request in her presence and in the presence of each other have hereunto subscribed our names as witnesses :

Susan Dora Cecilia Schintz

Kenneth Ewart
52 Bedford Square
London W.C.1
Solicitor

B. M. Ludkin
52 Bedford Square
London W.C.1
Secretary to Mr. K. Ewart.

Last will and testament of Dora Schintz.

EPILOGUE

Dora Schintz left behind several conundrums regarding herself and her life.

Why did she not marry? One might think that she would have been a very eligible woman having inherited much of her father's fortune. One could be forgiven for believing that the relationship between her and Rapson was more than that of just employer-employee. Rapson had access to her personal finances and acted on her behalf in many dealings and at one time had an apartment in the Mansion at Ottershaw while his wife lived in the family home in North London. Although there is no evidence that their relationship was anything other than platonic, it is difficult to explain why she spent the vast proportion of her fortune on him and defended his name to the last despite the fact that he had been, albeit unwittingly, instrumental in her financial downfall.

What was the reason behind her almost compulsive philanthropy? Female philanthropists historically gave of themselves in volunteer roles such as tending the sick and wounded or championing issues of social injustice, particularly those affecting women, children, and the poor. Dora, like her mother, was a keen supporter of this type of cause but the contribution of both mother and daughter was by way of financial donations. When Dora became extremely wealthy, her generosity knew no bounds. She funded a multitude of charities, gave generously to individuals, and sank her fortune into some misguided investments. Maybe it was just because she had the means, the time and the hunger for a social role that she took on the running of charities and gave generously to her less well-off fellows.

Why was she so keen on taking on legal battles? Dora was nothing if not litigious and her expenditure on court cases on many issues must have been enormous. Maybe it was just what one did at that time to resolve grievances before the appointment of ombudsmen and the like if one had the money?

The answers to these and many other questions that have so far eluded me may never be revealed.

ENDNOTES

1. 'Hackneys' are a breed of horse used for carriage driving and for showing in harness events and are characterised by their elegant high-stepping trot.
2. A formal description (blazon) of the Schintz coat of arms which means a blue (azure) shield with two silver or white (argent) ostrich feathers arising from a golden (or) crescent. A bar at the top of the shield (chief) bears a gold star (mullet…of the second [colour mentioned]) with six rays.
3. Alpine Club register, p. 252. The Alpine Society Archive.
4. Crypt. Wall. 5.345.
5. This is possibly a spelling error for Estancia El Descanso
6. *The Gentlewoman*, 25 April 1896. p.xvi
7. J. Wild, 2021. *History of Childwall*. Published privately.
8. *The Morning Post*, 11 July 1900. p.9
9. *Horses Illustrated*, 22 June 1907. p.9.
10. De Trafford, H.F. 1907. *The Horses of the British Empire*. University of Reading Library.
11. Leach, R.D., 2013., *Kenilworth People and Places* vol.2. p.137-144. Rookfield Publications.
12. *The British Architect*, 11 February 1910. p.3.

13 *Kenilworth Advertiser*, 30 March 1912. p.4.

14 *Hackney Horse Society Stud Book* vol. 28, p.102. Cambridge University Library P443.c.71

15 *Kenilworth Advertiser*, 22 August 1908. p.5.

16 Brocklebank, A.S. 2006. *The Road and the Ring*. p.55. Horse Drawn Carriages Ltd.

17 Bennett G.D.S., 1926. *Famous Harness Horses*. Vol. 1. pp.1, 19, 54-56, 75. British Library 7291.i.24.

18 *Runcorn Weekly News*, 22 October 1937. p.7.

19 *The Warwick and Warwickshire Advertiser*, 02 January 1915. p.2.

20 Mortgage of Thickthorn. ? 2506/5/18 check SHC

21 *The Times*, 04 September 1930.

22 Crypt. Wall. 5.343.

23 The main difference between these two faiths is that Catholics believe in the Trinity - Father, Son and Holy Ghost. Unitarians do not.

24 *Sheffield Daily Telegraph*, 15 April 1915. p.9.

25 *The Daily Sketch*, 10 December 1932.

26 *Chester Chronicle*, 17 August 1918. p.3.

27 *The British Journal of Nursing*, 09 February 1918, p.91.

28 During the First World War Voluntary Aid Detachment (VAD) nurses undertook essential tasks such as comforting and washing patients, cleaning bathrooms and other areas, dealing with bedpans, driving ambulances, and administrative duties.

29 *The Liverpool Echo*, 23 October 1916. p.3

30 *The Chester Chronicle*, 27 February 1915. p.7

31 *The Liverpool Echo*, 11 March 1915. p.6.

32 *The Birkenhead News*, 17 March 1915. p.3.

33 *Chester Chronicle*, 13 March 1915. p.8.

34 *Liverpool Home for Incurables*, Annual Reports, Miscellaneous Donations, 1912. Liverpool Record Office 614 PRI/9.

35 *The Liverpool Echo*, 20 June 1918, p.1; 25 June 1918, p.1; 19 July 1918, p.4.

36 For a full account of the life of F. L. Rapson refer to Clarke, T. and Athersuch, J., *Wrapped up in Rapson's Inventions*. The Flying Lady Jan/Feb and Mar/Apr2009.

37 *British Red Cross volunteers during WW1*. Website: https://vad.redcross.org.uk.

38 *The Star*, 10 October 1930.

39 For a complete history of Ottershaw Park Estate refer to Athersuch, J. 2018., *An Illustrated History of Ottershaw Park Estate* 1761- 2011. ISBN 978-1-904846-63-S.

40 A generic term for a labourer.

41 Burial no. 689, 20 February 1926. Christchurch Ottershaw archive.

42 Woking Crematorium reference no. 4795.

43 *Chancery Court Proceedings*, Case 1928 S. No. 3044, affidavit of Charles Taylor. TNA J4/10103.

44 It was common practice to purchase a vehicle chassis and have a body of your choice attached by coach builders such as Mulliner, Barker, Watson and Windovers.

45 *Abstract of title, with plan, to the Ottershaw Park estate, Chertsey, reciting from 1910 to 1929*. Surrey History Centre 6200/620.

46 *Chancery Court Proceedings*, Case 1931 S. No. 2935. TNA J54/2111, J4/10374, 10375, 10460-10463

47 *Auction brochure 1930*. Knight, Frank and Rutley. Chertsey Museum CHYMS 0135.3.

48 *Auction brochure 1930*. Gale Power & Co. Oliver Collection No. 1600. Royal Holloway University of London.

49 *Belfast Telegraph*, 1 August 1930. p.8.

50 *The London Gazette*, 25 July 1930. p.4694.

51 *The Daily Mail*, 10 December 1932.

52 *The Daily Mail*, 12 December 1932.

53 *The Courier-Mail* (Brisbane, Australia), 11 September 1933.

54 *Daily Gleaner*, 07 October 1933.
55 *The Evening Standard*, 07 September 1933.
56 Woking Crematorium reference no. 8798.
57 *The Daily Mirror*, 30 November 1936. p.1.
58 *Letter to Beatrice Burkly*, 05 July 1943.
59 *Letter to Betty Burkly*, 22 September 1946.
60 *Letter to Beatrice Burkly*, 14 January 1940.